POCKET BOOK OF
THE HUMAN BODY

First American Edition, 1987
Copyright © Kingfisher Books Ltd., 1986
All rights reserved including the right of reproduction in whole
or in part in any form

Published by Wanderer Books
A Division of Simon & Schuster, Inc.
Simon & Schuster Building
1230 Avenue of the Americas
New York, New York 10020

Wanderer and colophon are
trademarks of Simon & Schuster, Inc.

Also available in
Julian Messner Library Edition.

10   9   8   7   6   5   4   3   2   1

ISBN: 0-671-62973-5 (Pbk.)
ISBN: 0-671-63031-8 (Lib. Bdg.)

Edited and designed by Ann Kay
Cover Design: Pinpoint Design Company
Phototypeset by Southern Positives and
Negatives (SPAN), Lingfield, Surrey
Color separations by Newsele Litho, Milan
Printed in Portugal by Printer Portuguesa

SIMON & SCHUSTER'S
POCKET BOOK OF
THE HUMAN BODY

Brenda Walpole

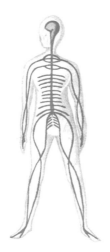

Medical Adviser: Dr. Peter Tanner

WANDERER BOOKS
Published by Simon & Schuster, Inc., New York

Contents

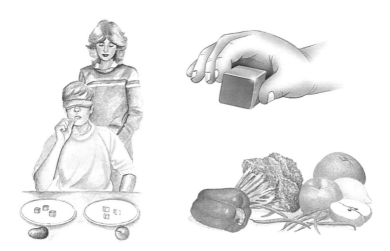

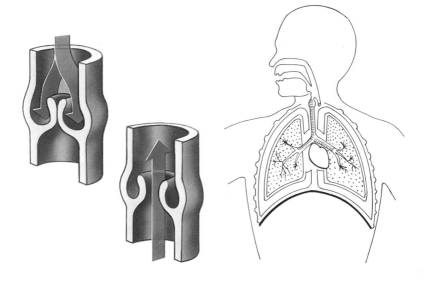

Introducing the Body

The human body – people often say that it would be difficult for us to invent such a complicated mechanism if we set out to. There are still things that we do not understand about how it works. This first section of the book deals with the body's basic structure – from the bones which form the body's scaffolding and the muscles which make us mobile, to the senses of smell, sight, touch, and hearing which make us aware of the outside world.

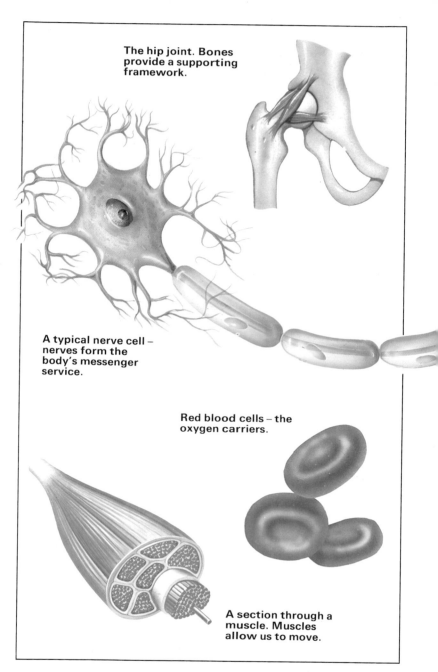

The hip joint. Bones provide a supporting framework.

A typical nerve cell – nerves form the body's messenger service.

Red blood cells – the oxygen carriers.

A section through a muscle. Muscles allow us to move.

9

Looking Inside

In order to understand how our bodies work, scientists have to be able to look inside. Here are some of the special instruments that they use to do this today.

Microscopes

Microscopes are used to magnify the cells of the human body so that we can study them, as they are much too small to be seen with the naked eye. A basic microscope that uses ordinary light magnifies objects by bending light rays with lenses. Usually two lenses are used – one close to the object and one close to the observer. To examine cells under a microscope, very thin slices of tissue are prepared and may be stained with dye. Each slice is then mounted onto a small piece of glass called a slide. Most microscopes have a light underneath the mounted specimen so that it can be seen clearly.

However, in the 1930s, the electron microscope was developed which can magnify far tinier objects than a light microscope. The principle is really the same except that it involves a beam of **electrons** – tiny charged particles – instead of ordinary light. Today it is electron microscopes that are usually used for looking at body cells. Certain photographs in this book are of electron microscope slides.

X rays

X rays are invisible waves of energy which can pass through most substances, including muscles and other soft parts of the body. However, some of the rays cannot pass through bone and so X-ray machines are used to look at the bones of the body. If a person stands in front of a photographic plate while being x-rayed, his or her bones cast a shadow on the plate. When the photo is developed a picture of the bones can be seen.

Endoscopes

These are instruments used by doctors to look inside a person's body. There are several different kinds of endoscopes. **Bronchoscopes** are used to examine the

▼ **An X-ray photograph** of a child's hand.

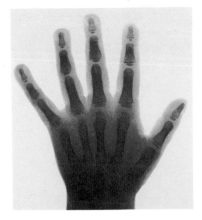

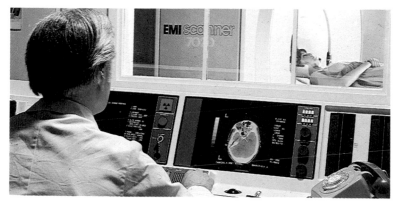

▲ **The body scanner machine** produces pictures that show far more detail than ordinary x-ray photographs. It x-rays a thin "slice" of the body from different angles and shows the picture on a screen.

bronchi and lungs. **Gastroscopes** look inside the stomach and intestines, and **arthroscopes** are used to examine the inside of joints.

An endoscope works by having a flexible "telescope" which can be gently pushed inside parts of the body. Light is transmitted down fine fibers of glass (a technique called fiber optics) to the viewing area and the image is carried back to the doctor's eye.

Ophthalmoscope

The ophthalmoscope is an instrument for looking inside the eye. Doctors use it to look through the pupil and see a wide area of the retina. A tiny lamp, powered by batteries in the handle of the ophthalmoscope, shines a light through the pupil

of the patient by means of a mirror or prism. The image which the doctor sees is magnified 15 times and is seen through a hole in the mirror. Using this, doctors can see any abnormalities in the eye. Some diseases, such as diabetes, may show themselves in the eye before symptoms appear anywhere else in the body.

▼ **Some ophthalmoscopes** can project a laser beam into the eye. This type is used to carry out laser surgery such as in the treatment of a detached retina.

11

Living Cells

Your body is made up of millions of tiny, living units called **cells.** Cells make up your blood, bones, skin, nerves, muscles, and all the other parts of your body.

All cells have the same basic structure, although they come in lots of different shapes and sizes. Each type of cell has its own special job to do.

INSIDE A CELL

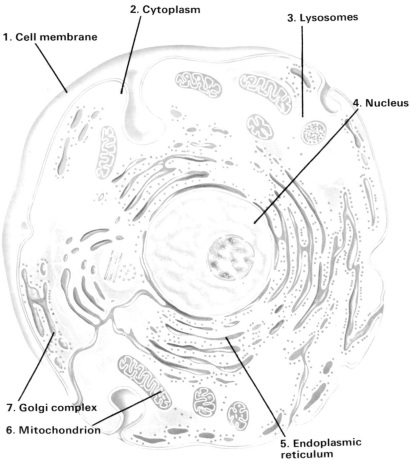

2. Cytoplasm

3. Lysosomes

1. Cell membrane

4. Nucleus

7. Golgi complex

6. Mitochondrion

5. Endoplasmic reticulum

PARTS OF THE CELL

1. Every cell has a **cell membrane** which encloses all its contents. The membrane is very thin and allows substances to pass through it. Food and oxygen can pass into the cell and substances made by the cell and any waste products can pass out.

2. **Cytoplasm** is the living "liquid" inside a cell. All the parts of the cell float in it. Chemicals which the cell needs to stay alive are dissolved in the cytoplasm.

3. **Lysosomes** are packets of digestive chemicals which can destroy harmful substances or worn-out parts of the cell.

4. The **nucleus** is the control center of the cell. It contains all the instructions the cell needs in the form of genes. Genes are made of a special chemical called DNA (see page 110). These instructions keep the cell alive and doing its own special job. Genes determine what each individual person looks like.

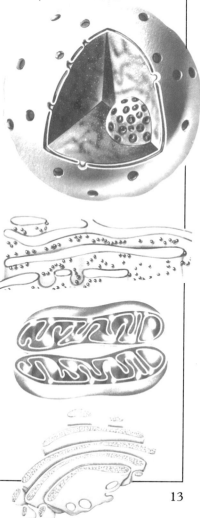

5. **Endoplasmic reticulum** is the folded, membrane-like structure in the cytoplasm. It acts as a system for transporting substances throughout the cell.

6. **Mitochondria** are the cell's powerhouses. It is here that energy needed to keep the cell working is released from food (glucose) and oxygen (see page 76).

7. The **golgi complex** is the flat arrangement of pockets where some substances are stored and others are prepared for use outside the cell.

Different Kinds of Cells

There are many sorts of cells in the human body. Some of the smallest cells are in the brain and measure only a fraction of an inch (0.005mm) across the cell body. The ovum or egg cell has the largest cell body with a diameter of 0.2mm – smaller than the period at the end of this sentence. Some cells are basically round, some are flat. A muscle cell has a long, cylindrical shape up to about $2\frac{1}{4}$ inches (60mm) in length.

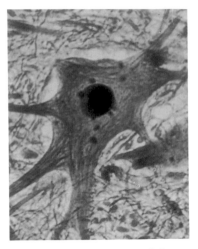

▼ **Various different kinds of cells** found in the body.

▲ **A microscope slide** of the body of a nerve cell in the spine.

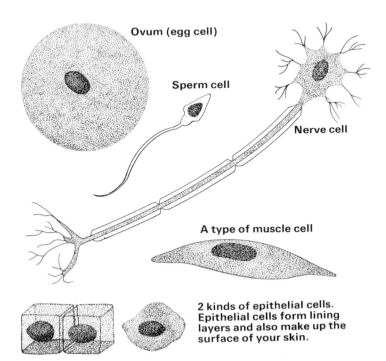

Ovum (egg cell)

Sperm cell

Nerve cell

A type of muscle cell

2 kinds of epithelial cells. Epithelial cells form lining layers and also make up the surface of your skin.

Tissues and Organs

Although each cell is an independent unit, cells often work together. A group of similar cells doing the same job is called a **tissue.** Muscles, bones, and nerves are three examples of different tissues.

Different types of tissue working together form **organs,** such as the heart, kidneys, or lungs. Groups of organs working together to perform a particular task are called **systems;** for example the blood (circulatory) system is responsible for organizing the flow of blood around your body.

How Long Do Cells Live?

Living cells grow and many of them **reproduce** themselves so that your body can grow larger and replace any dead or damaged cells. Some types of cells live for only a few days, while others last for weeks, months, or years. Bone cells last for about 15–20 years, while white blood cells last for only 4 months. Skin cells die after about 3 weeks. Nerve cells cannot reproduce at all and so are with you for most or all of your life.

HOW NEW CELLS ARE MADE

1. A single cell.
2. The cell grows larger.
3. Getting ready to divide.
4. Cell is dividing into two.
5. Division is complete – there are now two identical cells.

1

2
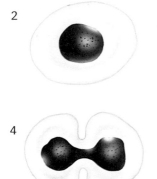

3

4

5

15

THE HUMAN SKELETON

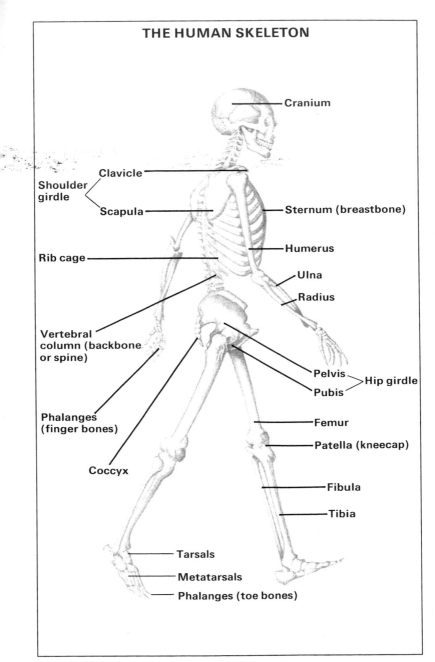

Cranium

Clavicle

Shoulder girdle

Scapula

Sternum (breastbone)

Rib cage

Humerus

Ulna

Radius

Vertebral column (backbone or spine)

Pelvis

Hip girdle

Pubis

Phalanges (finger bones)

Femur

Patella (kneecap)

Coccyx

Fibula

Tibia

Tarsals

Metatarsals

Phalanges (toe bones)

Special Scaffolding

Adults have about 206 bones in their **skeleton.** The number varies because some people have more bones in their hands and feet than others. The largest bone in the body is the thigh bone, or **femur,** and the smallest is a bone in the ear called the **stirrup.**

The skeleton provides a framework for your body, holding it together and supporting its weight. Muscles, which are responsible for our movement (see page 22), are attached to our bones.

Bones also protect important organs. The skull forms a bony case around the brain, the ribs form a cage around your heart and lungs, and the small bones called **vertebrae** (just one is called a **vertebra**), which make up your backbone, protect the spinal cord.

▲ 1. **The rib cage** protects the heart and lungs in the same way as the frame of an inspection lamp protects the delicate glass bulb inside.

▲ 2. **The hard skull** encloses the brain as the tough outer shell of a walnut protects the soft nut inside.

DID YOU KNOW?

✳ A giraffe has the same number of vertebrae in its neck as you do, although its neck is much longer.

✳ There are 29 bones in your skull. This includes all the bones in your face and the 3 small bones inside your ear.

✳ Some people suffer from a condition called **rickets**. This is caused by not having enough calcium and Vitamin D in your diet when your bones are developing. It makes bones stay soft and become bent and deformed.

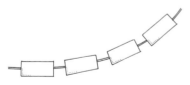

◄ 3. **The vertebrae** are arranged along the spinal cord rather like a string of beads.

17

Where Bones Meet

Bones cannot bend, but where two bones meet, they form a **joint.** This usually allows us to bend, twist, or turn our bodies.

At a joint, the bones are held together by strong elastic straps called **ligaments** and by muscles. The ends of the bones are covered with a soft but tough tissue called **cartilage** to prevent the bones from grinding against each other. Also, a liquid called **synovial fluid** provides lubrication, rather like oil does to a hinge.

If a joint is twisted too far, the ligaments may tear, causing a **sprain.** If the joint is pulled out of place, it is said to be **dislocated.**

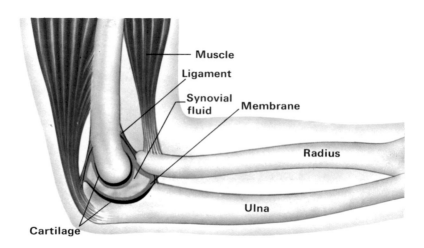

Muscle

Ligament

Synovial fluid

Membrane

Radius

Ulna

Cartilage

▲ **The elbow joint.** A joint is where two or more bones meet. Ligaments hold the bones together, and cartilage and synovial fluid allow movement.

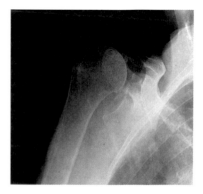

▶ **An X-ray photograph of a dislocated shoulder**, where the upper bone of the arm – the humerus – has been pulled out of its socket in the shoulder girdle (see page 16).

18

DIFFERENT KINDS OF JOINTS

There are several different types of joints in the human body, some of which are shown below. Each kind allows a different type of movement. Look at these examples and compare them by moving some of the joints in your own body.

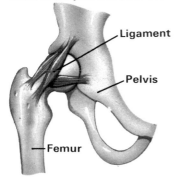

Ligament
Pelvis
Femur

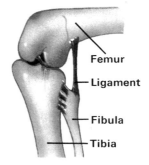

Femur
Ligament
Fibula
Tibia

▲ **Ball and socket** joints can move in a complete circle. Examples are the shoulders and hips.

▲ **Hinge** joints can only move in one direction, like a door hinge. You can find hinge joints at the knee, the elbow, and between the bones in your fingers.

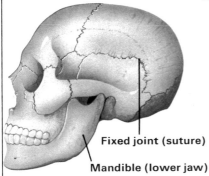

Fixed joint (suture)
Mandible (lower jaw)

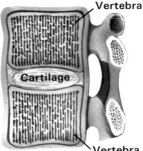

Vertebra
Cartilage
Vertebra

▲ **The skull** is made of several bones, but the places where they join fuse together when we are very young so that the joints are **fixed** ones – they do not move. The lower jaw is the only part of the skull that moves.

▲ **The spine** is so flexible because it is a whole series of **vertebral** joints. Between each pair of vertebrae a disk of cartilage cushions against any jarring. Sometimes, a disk slips out of place, pressing painfully against a nerve. This is called having a **slipped disk**.

Inside a Bone

Bones may seem dry and lifeless, but they are very much alive. The outer layer of bone is hard **compact** bone which consists of living bone cells forming rings around tiny canals called **Haversian** canals. Inside each canal there are blood vessels which carry food and oxygen to the bone cells. The compact bone is in turn covered with a tough layer called the **periosteum.**

The inner part of the bone looks like a honeycomb and forms a very strong network of bone cells with spaces in between. This part is often called **spongy** bone, but it is just as strong as the compact bone.

In the center of many bones

HOW BROKEN BONES MEND

Because bone cells are alive, they can grow and reproduce so that the new cells close up any breaks. If the two broken ends are lined up and held still, inside a plaster cast for example, the bone will heal and be as straight and strong as it was originally. The healing process usually takes about 12 weeks for bones such as those in the leg or arm.

1. A bone is broken in the arm.

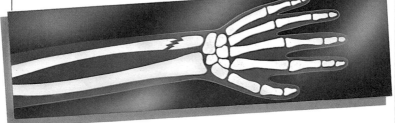

2. A blood clot (see page 34) forms to seal the space between the broken ends.

3. About two days later bone cells from the periosteum move in and grow and divide to seal the gap with new bone.

4. If the bones are held in place, the new bone will grow into the correct shape. Eventually, no bump should be left at the join.

there is bone **marrow.** Marrow is a fatty substance which can manufacture up to 5 billion red blood cells each day. It also makes the white blood cells (see page 94).

Bones also store minerals such as calcium and phosphorus, which the body can use when they are needed. It is these minerals that make bones hard.

INSIDE A BONE

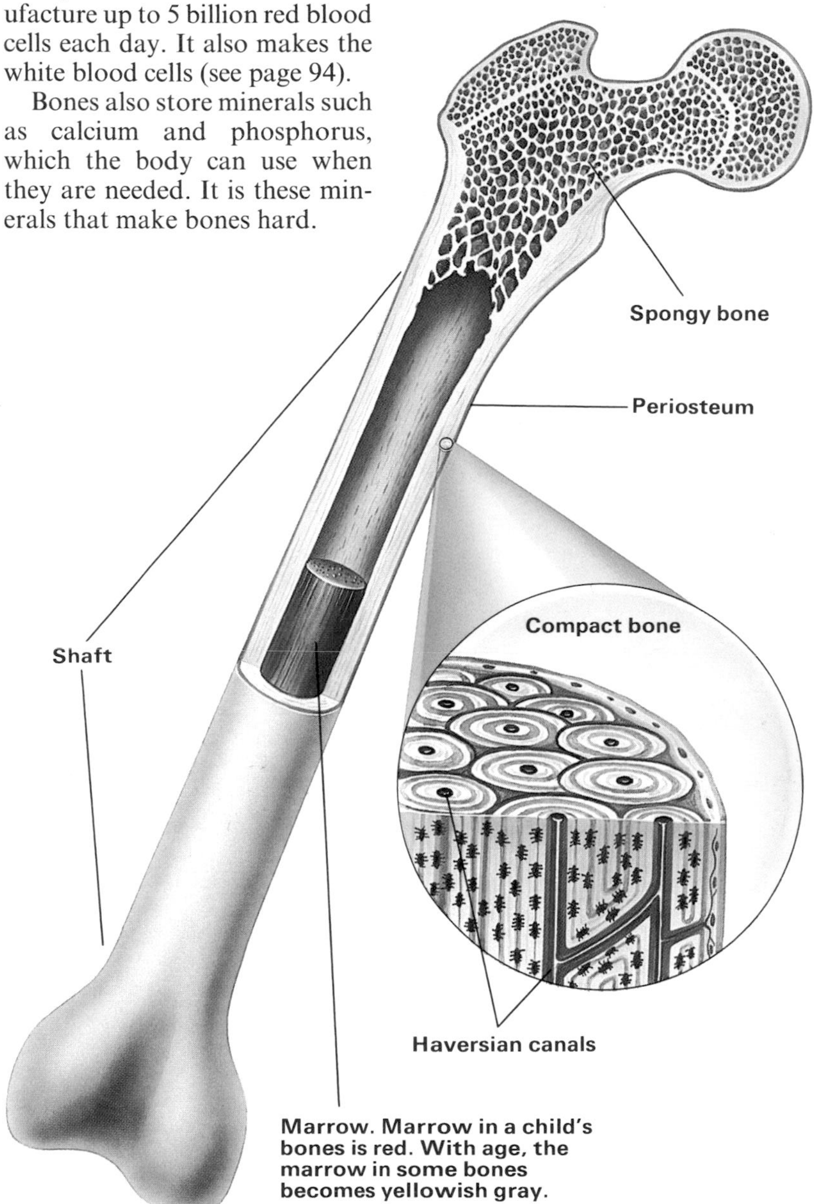

Spongy bone

Periosteum

Compact bone

Shaft

Haversian canals

Marrow. Marrow in a child's bones is red. With age, the marrow in some bones becomes yellowish gray.

21

How You Move

Joints allow your bones to move, but your muscles cause the actual movement so that you can walk, write, close your eyes, or smile. Muscles are attached to your bones by **tendons.** When muscles contract, they pull your bones and you can move your body. Muscles contract when they receive messages from your nerves (see page 42).

Most muscles are long and thin and made up of many fibers – muscle cells – arranged in bundles (see page 25). Usually one end of a muscle is attached to one side of a joint and the other end to the other side. Muscles can only pull, they cannot push. That is why most muscles come in pairs and work together. You can see how in the diagram below. But not all muscles have a long, thin shape. The diaphragm, which is used for breathing, is a flat sheet of muscle. Other muscles are in layers. There are three layers of muscles across your abdomen which protect the tissues and organs underneath.

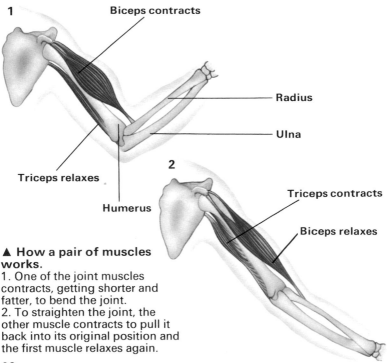

1
Biceps contracts

Radius

Ulna

Triceps relaxes

2

Triceps contracts

Biceps relaxes

Humerus

▲ **How a pair of muscles works.**
1. One of the joint muscles contracts, getting shorter and fatter, to bend the joint.
2. To straighten the joint, the other muscle contracts to pull it back into its original position and the first muscle relaxes again.

As well as being arranged in different shapes, there are different kinds of muscle tissue. One kind of muscle moves food along the digestive system, as well as doing other jobs in the body. Another type of muscle keeps the heart beating. Muscles doing these kinds of jobs work automatically, and because we cannot control what they do just by thinking about it, they are called **involuntary** muscles. Muscles which we can control by thinking about them are called **voluntary** or **skeletal** muscles. The muscles in your arms and legs are examples of skeletal muscles.

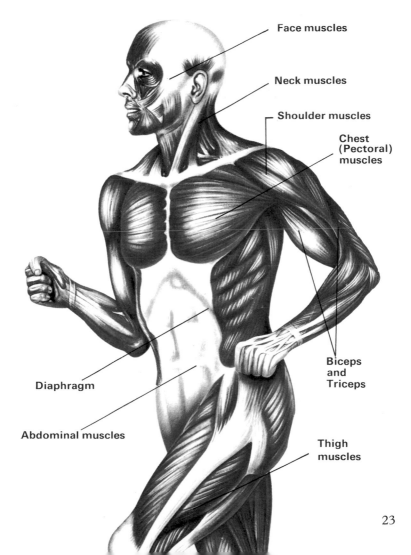

Face muscles

Neck muscles

Shoulder muscles

Chest (Pectoral) muscles

Biceps and Triceps

Diaphragm

Abdominal muscles

Thigh muscles

Different Kinds of Muscles

The type of muscle that moves your arms and legs – **striped** (**skeletal**) muscle – is made of many long cells. Each one of these cells (or fibers) contains many nuclei (one is called a nucleus) and looks striped. Each cell in heart – **cardiac** – muscle has only one nucleus. These cells are shorter and less striped than those in skeletal muscle. **Smooth** muscle, which does work in many of the body's internal systems, such as moving food down your digestive system, has short, unstriped cells, each with only one nucleus.

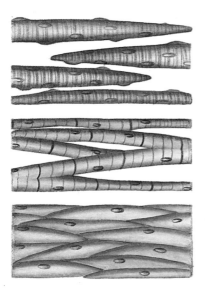

◀ **Striped (skeletal) muscle.** The cells are long and striped, with several nuclei in each cell.

◀ **Heart (cardiac) muscle.** The cells are shorter and less striped than those in skeletal muscle. There is one nucleus in each cell.

◀ **Smooth muscle.** Short, unstriped cells with one nucleus in each cell.

Muscle cells can shorten by up to one third of their length. When they contract they always shorten as far as they can. If all the cells in a muscle shorten at the same time, the result is a jerky movement, for example when you pull your hand away from a hot object. Usually muscle cells contract in sequence and so the muscle moves smoothly. Several muscles working together let us make very precise movements.

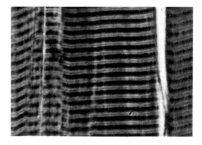

▲ **Striped muscle** under the microscope. The stripes are caused by bands of two different proteins in the muscle fibers.

INSIDE A SKELETAL MUSCLE

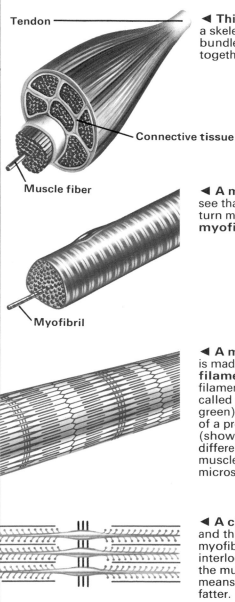

Tendon

Connective tissue

Muscle fiber

Myofibril

◀ **This diagram shows** that a skeletal muscle is made up of bundles of fibers (cells) held together by connective tissue.

◀ **A muscle fiber.** You can see that each muscle fiber is in turn made up of strands called **myofibrils**.

◀ **A myofibril.** Each myofibril is made up of two types of **filaments**. There are thick filaments made of a protein called **myosin** (shown in green) and thin filaments made of a protein called **actin** (shown in red). It is these two different proteins that make the muscle look striped under the microscope.

◀ **A clearer view** of the thick and thin filaments in a myofibril. When these interlocking filaments overlap, the muscle contracts, which means that it gets shorter and fatter.

Using Muscles and Keeping Fit

To keep your muscles fit and strong, you need exercise. This will not give you more muscles, but it can increase the size of the ones you have. Without exercise, muscles shrink. This can happen when you are ill and have to stay in bed for a long time.

To keep your muscles working properly, you need a good diet. Protein is important. It builds up muscle cells and is used to repair them if they get damaged. Sugars, for example glucose, are important in providing muscles with energy. Muscles use oxygen to release energy (see page 76). Also, muscles produce heat when they use energy, which is why you get hot when you exercise. The harder the muscles work, the more energy they need, which explains why you pant and your heart beats faster as you exercise – your body is working to supply muscles with extra food and oxygen.

Sometimes, the muscles do not receive enough glucose and oxygen when they are working really hard. Then they start to release energy from their own stores of glucose without oxygen. This produces a waste substance called **lactic acid** which makes muscles tired and they begin to ache. Also, if your muscles are being strained, they may stay contracted for too long. When this happens, the muscle is said to be "in spasm." This is also called **cramp** and it can be very painful. You can help to prevent this by exercising regularly and by building up to any exercise gradually. This is why people have gentle "warm up" sessions before many forms of exercise. Muscles are less likely to cramp up if they are kept warm. Most dancers wear garments such as leg warmers at the beginning of practice sessions for this reason.

▶ **Regular exercise** is very important for keeping your muscles in good shape.

DID YOU KNOW?

✳ Muscles account for 40% of your total body weight.

✳ You use over 200 different muscles when you walk.

✳ Even when you are not moving, some of your muscle fibers have to contract to keep you standing up or sitting down.

Your Blood System

Blood, pumped by your **heart** (see page 31) travels all around your body in a network, or system, of vessels. There are three main types of blood vessels. **Arteries** take blood containing food and oxygen from the heart to the cells of the body. Blood in the arteries is under high pressure, traveling rapidly, so the walls of these vessels are thick and muscular. Arteries divide into smaller and smaller vessels. The tiniest of these are called **capillaries**, the smallest blood vessels in the body. Capillaries fit between the body's cells and so can easily deliver food and oxygen to them and collect their waste products. Eventually capillaries join up to form **veins.** These take back to the heart blood which has had all its oxygen used up by the body's cells. Veins have thinner, less firm walls than arteries as blood in them travels at low pressure.

What is Blood?

Blood is made up of **red cells, white cells,** and tiny bits of cells called **platelets,** all floating in a yellow liquid called **plasma.**

Red blood cells are small, round, and flexible, so that they can squeeze through the tiniest capillaries. They are made in the marrow of the bones, have no nucleus, and do not live for more than a few weeks. These red cells contain a substance called **hemoglobin,** which "carries" oxygen to all parts of the body. Hemoglobin gives red cells their color and so makes our blood look red.

There are several different kinds of white blood cells. They are made in the bone marrow, like the red cells. Most white blood cells are larger than the red cells and their main job is to fight disease (see page 94).

Plasma is mostly water with some proteins and salts. It carries digested food to your cells and collects their waste products. Platelets help to heal any wounds that you may have (see page 34).

▼ **Your blood consists of** red blood cells, white blood cells, and platelets floating in a liquid called plasma.

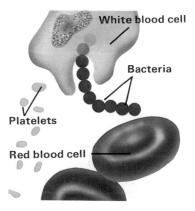

White blood cell

Bacteria

Platelets

Red blood cell

▶ **The main vessels** of the blood or circulatory system. Arteries (shown in red) take blood containing food and oxygen from the heart to the cells of the body. Veins (shown in blue) carry blood back to the heart. The heart is the pump which powers the whole blood system.

▼ **Various arteries and veins,** shown at about their actual size. A capillary is even smaller than the full stop at the end of this sentence.

The aorta – the largest artery in the body

Artery

Arteriole

Venule

Vein

Vena cava

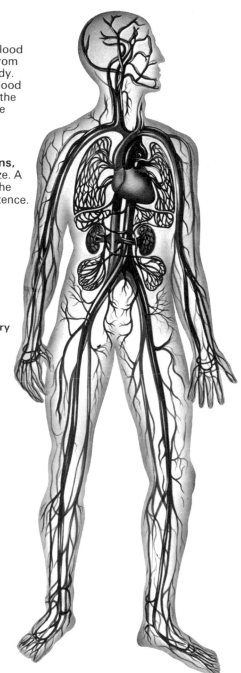

Your Heart

Your heart is inside your chest, protected by the ribs and breast bone. It is about the same size as your clenched fist and weighs roughly 10½ ounces (300 grams) in an average adult. The heart is made of strong cardiac muscle and constantly pumps blood around your body, so that each cell gets the food and oxygen it needs. The body cannot stay alive for longer than about five minutes if the heart stops working completely.

The heart is divided into four chambers – the left and right **atria** (one is called an **atrium**) and the left and right **ventricles.** The network of veins carrying blood (low in oxygen) from the cells of the body join up to form two very large veins – the **venae cavae** (one is called the **superior vena cava** and the other is the **inferior vena cava**). The venae cavae go to the right atrium. The right atrium pumps blood through a **valve** (see diagram below) into the right ventricle. From there the blood is pumped through a second valve into the **pulmonary artery.** "Pulmonary" means to do with the lungs, and the pulmonary artery links the heart to the lungs, where the blood collects oxygen.

Pulmonary veins bring blood back from the lungs to the left side of your heart. From the left atrium, blood is pumped through a third valve into the left ventricle. The left ventricle pumps blood out of the heart, through a fourth valve, and into your main artery – the **aorta** – from where it travels around your body. Heart cells get their own blood supply from the **coronary arteries,** which branch off the aorta to form a network over the surface of the heart.

VALVES in your heart stop blood flowing backward. Many large veins have valves too, as blood there is at low pressure and could easily flow backward. The valves shown below are the type found in veins and between ventricles and arteries.

◀ **Blood flowing forward** forces valve flaps open.

▶ **Blood flowing backward** forces flaps to close.

INSIDE THE HEART

Areas shown in red indicate where oxygen-rich blood travels.

Areas shown in blue indicate where blood low in oxygen travels.

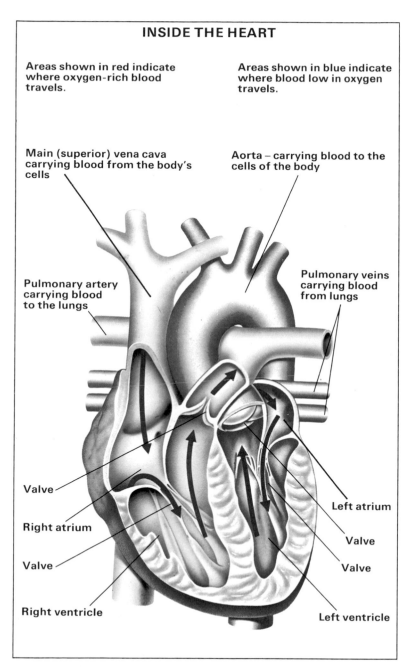

Main (superior) vena cava carrying blood from the body's cells

Aorta – carrying blood to the cells of the body

Pulmonary artery carrying blood to the lungs

Pulmonary veins carrying blood from lungs

Valve

Right atrium

Valve

Right ventricle

Left atrium

Valve

Valve

Left ventricle

Heartbeat

When blood is pumped out of the heart's chambers, the valves flap shut. The sound of a **heartbeat** is the sound of these valves closing. The complete heartbeat cycle takes less than one second. The two atria contract together and so do the two ventricles. The "thump-thump" that you can hear if you put your ear to someone's chest is first the valves inside the heart closing and then the valves in the aorta and pulmonary artery snapping shut. A **stethoscope** – the instrument used by doctors to listen to your heartbeat – makes these sounds easier to hear.

Your **heart rate** is the number of times your heart beats in one minute. An adult's heart beats about 70 times each minute. Children have a faster rate. Heart rate is controlled by the brain, which sends messages through nerves to the heart. Hormones can also speed up the heart rate. Your heart rate increases when you are very active and your muscles need extra blood. It also increases after you have had a meal. This is because more blood is pumped to your digestive system to cope with the process of carrying the food away to all of the body's cells (see page 72).

FIND OUT YOUR OWN HEART RATE

Doctors may use stethoscopes to measure heart rate, but you can find out your own heart rate by feeling your **pulse**. Each time your heart beats, blood rushes through your arteries at high pressure, causing them to throb, or pulsate. The inside of your wrist is a good place to feel your pulse because the blood vessels are close to the surface.

▶ **Feel the inside of one of your wrists** with the fingertips of the other hand. The best place to feel is toward the edge of your wrist, in line with your thumb, where there is a main artery. Use your watch to count the number of beats in one minute.

Try measuring your heart rate when you are doing various things that require different amounts of energy. Jot down the rates and compare them.

HEART RATE
After running...
After lunch.....
After a walk.....
Watching T.V......

Blood Groups

There are four different blood groups – **A, B, AB,** and **O.** Your group depends on substances – **factors A** and **B** – on your red blood cells. Also, different blood groups have different combinations of two substances called **antibody A** and **antibody B** in their plasma. The antibodies in the plasma of one blood group can react against the factors on the red cells of another blood group. Because of this, when people are given blood **transfusions,** they must receive blood which matches with their own type or their body may reject it.

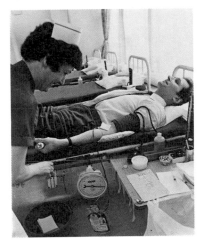

▲ **A blood donor** giving blood at a special center. The whole process of giving blood only takes about an hour.

Giving Blood

Hospitals need to have a supply of blood ready for operations and emergencies. People who volunteer to give some of their own blood at special centers are called **blood donors.** An average healthy adult can usually manage to give a small amount of blood without feeling any effects. Blood donors give about $\frac{3}{4}$ of a pint (400cc) of blood from a vein in the arm. This blood is kept in a sterile bag with a substance called sodium citrate which stops blood clotting. Blood can be stored like this for about ten days if it is kept cool at about 41°F (5°C), or longer if glucose is added. Before blood is given to people who need it, it is warmed to body temperature.

BLOOD GROUPS

BLOOD GROUP	CONTAINS ANTIBODIES WHICH REACT AGAINST	CAN GIVE BLOOD TO	CAN RECEIVE BLOOD FROM
A	B	A or AB	O, A
B	A	B or AB	O, B
AB	no antibodies against other blood groups	AB	A, B, AB, O
O	A & B	A, B, AB, O	O

What Can Go Wrong with the Blood System?

Both veins and arteries have flexible walls and a smooth lining when they are healthy. However, as people get older, the artery walls may harden and deposits of calcium and a fatty substance called cholesterol (see page 69) may appear inside the vessels, rather like fur inside a pipe. These deposits leave less room for the blood to flow through and pressure can build up in the vessels, sometimes causing them to burst. High blood pressure can be caused by stress, but there is still a lot that we do not understand about this.

Another problem occurs when blood clots form in narrow, hardened blood vessels. If these clots block the vessels and cut off the blood supply to cells, the cells may die. This can cause a heart attack (see Medical Facts opposite). People can help to prevent heart attacks by having a healthy diet with a minimum of cholesterol and by getting plenty of exercise. This helps to stop the blood vessels from becoming blocked and keeps the heart muscle in good condition.

How a Wound Heals

When you bump yourself against something hard, you may cause a **bruise.** Blood vessels under the skin have broken and the blood leaking out makes a blue or black mark – the bruise.

When you cut yourself, your skin breaks too and blood from the broken vessels leaks out onto the surface of your skin. Any leaks in vessels or skin need to be stopped quickly so that you do not lose too much blood. To do this, your blood **clots** to plug the gap.

▼ **Blood leaks** through cut skin from broken blood vessels. A **clot** forms as platelets collect around the cut and threads of a substance called **fibrin** develop.

▼ **A web of fibrin** traps blood cells and platelets and dries to form a scab. This protects the cut from bacteria and stops the bleeding.

▼ **Under the scab,** new skin has been growing over the cut. When the scab drops off, the skin underneath should be almost healed.

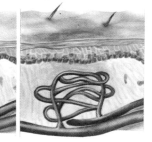

* There is another substance, apart from factors A and B, that is carried by some people's red blood cells. This is called the **Rhesus factor**. It was named after the kind of monkey in which it was first found. People who have this factor are said to be **Rhesus positive – Rh +**. Those without it are called **Rhesus negative – Rh −**. This is another thing that must be considered when giving blood transfusions.

* An adult's body contains over 8 pints (about 5 liters) of blood.

* a few drops (1cc) of blood contain about 5 billion red blood cells and about 11 million white cells.

* **Plasma** is blood minus platelets, red cells or white cells. **Serum** is plasma minus any clotting agents.

MEDICAL FACTS

● A **stroke** can occur when brain cells do not receive enough oxygen because the blood vessels in the brain are blocked or have burst.

● A **heart attack** or **coronary** can be caused by a blood clot blocking the coronary arteries so that some of the heart cells die. Heart cells can also die if they are diseased.

● If blood starts going the wrong way in the body's veins because the valves there are not working properly, the veins become swollen and painful. This is known as having **varicose veins**.

● A person may faint if his or her blood pressure falls and not enough blood reaches the brain. This can happen, for example, when a person is suffering from extreme stress or blood loss.

● **Blood poisoning** can occur when a lot of bacteria get into a person's bloodstream.

● People who suffer from **hemophilia** have blood that cannot clot properly. They can bleed to death from a tiny cut or small bruise.

Skin

Skin protects your body from the outside world. It encloses you in a waterproof, flexible covering and helps to keep out harmful bacteria. Your skin enables you to sense what is happening around you because it is sensitive to touch, heat, cold, and pain. It helps to protect you from strong sunlight and uses some sunlight to make vitamin D (see page 68).

There are two main layers to your skin. The outer layer, which you can see, is called the **epidermis** and the layer underneath that is known as the **dermis.**

UNDER THE SKIN

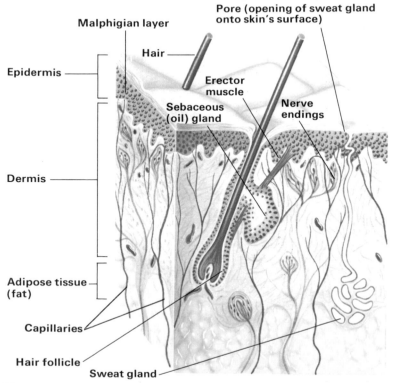

Pore (opening of sweat gland onto skin's surface)

Malphigian layer

Hair

Epidermis

Erector muscle

Sebaceous (oil) gland

Nerve endings

Dermis

Adipose tissue (fat)

Capillaries

Hair follicle

Sweat gland

▲ **Skin color** varies enormously because of melanin, a pigment which protects skin from the sun's harmful rays. This is why people "tan" in bright sunlight and also why people from hot and sunny climates usually have darker skin than those from colder climates.

The skin that you can see is made of the dead cells of the epidermis. New cells are made at the bottom of the epidermis in the **malphigian layer.** The new cells push the older cells upward, toward the surface. By the time cells reach the surface, they are dead and compressed into a flat shape. These dead cells contain a substance called **keratin,** which makes them hard so that they form a strong covering. Dead cells are continually worn off the surface of your skin.

The malphigian layer also produces a colored substance (a pigment) called **melanin.** People with a lot of melanin have dark skin and those with only a little have fair skin. Melanin protects the skin from the sun's harmful rays. In bright sunlight, extra melanin is produced to cope, and the skin may turn a darker color.

The lower layer of your skin, the dermis, contains nerves, blood vessels, hair roots, and glands. Different nerves respond to heat, cold, pressure, and pain (see page 62). Below the dermis is a layer of fat, or **adipose tissue,** which provides insulation and a store of food. Adipose tissue is thicker on some parts of the body than on others. For example, it is thicker around the thighs than around the ankles. Women tend to deposit more fat than men.

Keeping Warm and Cooling Off

One of the most important jobs the skin has is helping to keep your body at the correct temperature (see Medical Facts on opposite page). Blood vessels, hairs, and sweat glands in the skin work together automatically all the time to keep you warm on cold days and cool on hot days.

Because the body can keep a constant temperature inside, people are able to live in very different climates. We can help to maintain our body temperature in various ways. In cold weather we can wear lots of clothes to trap layers of warm air around our body and in hot weather we can drink a lot to replace body fluids lost through sweating.

Sweating is also a way of getting rid of some of the body's waste products (see page 82). Sweat glands can react to feelings so that nervous people sweat more than others. You have many sweat glands under your arms and on the palms of your hands.

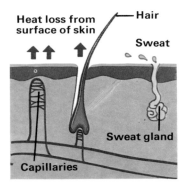
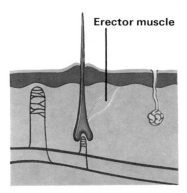

▲ When You Are Hot . . . . .

● Sweat glands produce more sweat – mainly water with salts and various other substances dissolved in it – which evaporates from the skin, taking heat away with it.

● Blood vessels widen and carry more warm blood to the surface, where the air outside your body can cool it.

● Your hairs lie flat so that there is no warm air trapped between them.

▲ When You Are Cold . . . . .

● You do not sweat.

● Blood vessels narrow.

● Erector muscles contract to make your hairs stand up, which traps warm air between them. You see this effect as "goosepimples" on your skin. Also, the rest of your muscles automatically contract, producing a little heat as they do so and making you "shiver."

38

✳ Wrinkles appear as skin gets older and becomes thinner, drier, and less elastic.

✳ Skin is about $\frac{1}{25}$ inch (1mm) thick on your eyelids, $\frac{1}{8}$ inch (3mm) thick on the palms of your hands and the soles of your feet, and about $\frac{1}{12}$ inch (2mm) thick elsewhere.

✳ Freckles are an uneven distribution of melanin in the epidermis.

✳ Fingerprints are patterns in the dermis. No two people have exactly the same pattern, which is why they are useful for crime detection. Even if the outer layers of skin are damaged, fingerprints are not altered. (Also see Glossary.)

✳ Spots on the skin are caused by too much sebum (see page 40) blocking the pores or follicles.

MEDICAL FACTS

°F	°C	
		Unconsciousness, possibly death
106	41	Heat stroke / Pulse rate rises
100	37.7	Fever
99	37.2	Normal body temperature
97	36	
95	35	Shivering
93	34	Pulse rate falls
86	30	Unconsciousness
82	28	Respiration stops
77	25	Death

The average or "normal" temperature inside the human body is 98·6°F (37°C), though different people may have normal temperatures that are very slightly higher or lower than this. Maintaining a constant body temperature is vital as people can be very ill if their temperature goes up or down by just a few degrees.

A HAIR FOLLICLE

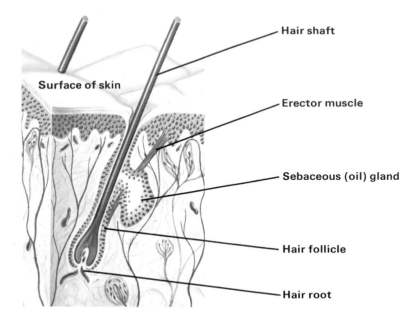

Hair shaft

Surface of skin

Erector muscle

Sebaceous (oil) gland

Hair follicle

Hair root

Hair

Hairs grow out from roots in the dermis layer of the skin. They are found all over your body, although more grow in some places than others.

Each hair root is enclosed in its own **follicle,** which has a blood supply, a tiny **erector** muscle and a gland. The gland produces an oily substance called **sebum,** which lubricates the hair and the skin around it. Too much sebum causes greasy hair. The erector muscle can pull the hair upright. This happens when you are cold (see page 38).

Only the base of each hair is alive. New cells which are produced at the base push older cells upward so that the hair grows longer. The growth of hair is controlled by hormones (see page 88). At puberty, hair begins to grow under the arms and around the genitals, and boys develop a beard on their chin. Later in life, as changes happen to the hormones in the body, hairs may stop growing and a person may become bald. The type of hair you have and the tendency to go bald are inherited characteristics which run in families.

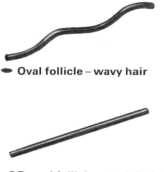

Oval follicle – wavy hair

Round follicle – straight hair

Flat follicle – curly hair

▲ **The type of hair you have** depends partly on the shape of your hair follicles.

Nails

Nails are made of dead cells which contain keratin, the tough protein which makes up your hair and the outer layer of your skin. Each nail grows from a nail-bed which is overlapped by a fold of skin called the **cuticle.** The "half moons" at the base of your nails look white because this part is not firmly attached to the skin below.

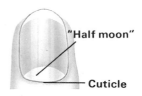

"Half moon"

Cuticle

▲ **Fingernails** are made of keratin and grow about $\frac{1}{50}$ inch (0.5 mm) each week.

DID YOU KNOW?

✳ Hair on your head grows about $\frac{1}{2}$ inch (12mm) each month and most hairs can grow to a length of about $27\frac{1}{2}$ inches (700mm) before they fall out.

✳ About 50 hairs fall from your head each day.

✳ A hair follicle rests for about three months after a hair has fallen out before a new hair grows from it.

✳ Hair color is an inherited characteristic. It depends on the amount of melanin (the same pigment that determines skin color) in special cells at the base of each hair follicle. A little melanin produces fair hair, a lot produces darker hair.

41

The Nervous System

Your nervous system is like a control system for the body, making sure that all its different parts work together efficiently. A complex network of **nerves** (bundles of the long fibers of nerve cells) collects information from both inside and outside your body and sends messages to the brain. The messages travel along the nerve fibers in the form of electrical impulses. Your brain processes the information it receives and acts on some of it by sending messages back along the nerves to tell the body what to do. Some of the information received by the brain is stored as **memory** for future use.

As you sit and read this book, your brain is organizing, or co-ordinating, the way your eyes see the words on the page, how your hands are holding the book, and the way you are sitting in the chair. It is also taking care of other vital jobs such as making sure that your heart keeps beating, your lungs are expanding and contracting, and your body temperature is at the right level. It is because of your nervous system that you know where you are and what you are doing.

Parts of the Nervous System
The nervous system can be divided into two parts. First, your brain and spinal cord together are known as the **central nervous system.** The spinal cord carries messages to and from your brain and your body.

The rest of the system consists of the nerves coming out of the brain and spinal cord. These nerves make up the outer, or **peripheral nervous system.** There are two kinds of fibers in most of the peripheral nerves. One kind belongs to **sensory** nerve cells, which carry messages from your skin and sense organs to the central nervous system. The other fibers are those of **motor** nerve cells, which carry messages back from the central nervous system to the muscles. Sensory and motor nerve cells are linked in the central nervous system by special **connector** nerve cells and allow you to deal with the outside world.

Autonomic Nervous System
Many peripheral nerves also contain the fibers of nerve cells which carry messages to and from the organs and glands inside your body. These cells form the **autonomic nervous system.** They connect the major systems of the body such as the blood, digestive, respiratory, and reproductive systems to two special parts of the brain – the **brain stem** and the **hypothalamus.** These areas direct automatic (autonomic) activities, such as digestion, which we cannot consciously control.

THE NERVOUS SYSTEM

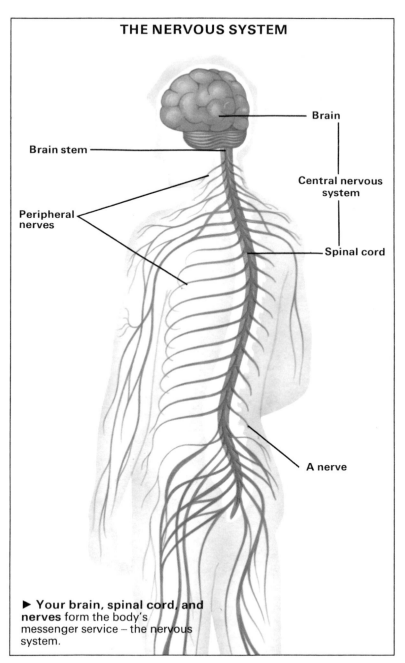

Brain

Brain stem

Central nervous system

Peripheral nerves

Spinal cord

A nerve

▶ Your brain, spinal cord, and **nerves** form the body's messenger service – the nervous system.

43

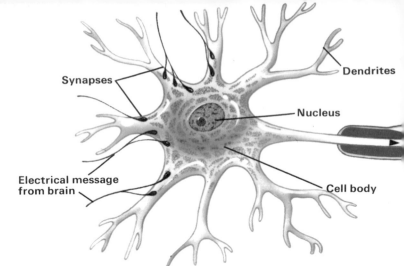

Synapses

Dendrites

Nucleus

Electrical message from brain

Cell body

Sending Messages

Nerve cells are often called **neurons.** A typical neuron has a cell body with fibers branching from it. Short fibers called **dendrites** carry messages in the form of electrical impulses to the cell body. One long fiber, called an **axon,** carries messages away from the cell body to the dendrites of other neurons. It is bundles of axons that make up the peripheral nerves. Many axons are wrapped in a fatty substance called **myelin.** This covering helps to stop electrical messages from escaping. Electrical wires have a covering – insulation – around them for the same reason.

Much of the brain and spinal cord are made of neurons. In the spine and brain, the cell bodies of neurons make up an area called **gray matter** and their axons form **white matter.** Axons vary in length and some are extremely long – the longest neuron in the body runs from the spinal cord to the toes. It can be up to $4\frac{1}{4}$ feet (1.3 meters) long.

Getting the Message Across
A typical message in the nervous system starts its journey when the sensitive axon endings of a sensory neuron are stimulated. The axon endings of certain kinds of neurons are called **receptors** (see page 62). They can be stimulated mechanically (for example by touch) or chemically (for example by a smell).

Neurons do not touch one another, so a message passing from the axon of one cell to a dendrite of the next cell must cross a gap. This gap is called a **synapse.** A message cannot cross a synapse in the form of an electrical impulse, so it crosses in the form of a chemical. The bran-

A MOTOR NERVE CELL

Axon

Path of electrical message

Myelin sheath

ching ends of axons have little knobs on them. These knobs contain a special chemical called a **neurotransmitter.** When an electrical impulse reaches a knob, it causes the neurotransmitter to be released. This chemical then crosses the synapse to a dendrite of the next neuron. When a certain amount of neurotransmitter has built up at the dendrite, an electrical impulse is produced and the message continues its journey.

Messages pass from one neuron to another very rapidly – the whole process only takes a fraction of a second. As there are many millions of neurons in your body, the number of possible pathways between them is almost endless.

Axon endings

Muscle

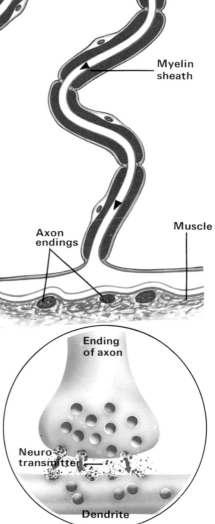

Ending of axon

Neuro- transmitter

Dendrite

▶ **A synapse** – where messages pass from one neuron to another.

Reflex Actions

Every day you make a lot of decisions and choose to do many different things. When the front door bell rings, messages from sensory organs, in this case your ears, travel to your brain. If you decide that you want to open the door, your brain sends messages to your muscles so that you can walk to the door, turn the handle, and open it.

But you do some things without thinking about them at all. For example, if your hand touches something very hot, it will jerk away almost immediately. This kind of action is called a **reflex action.** Reflexes are automatic responses, most of which are controlled by your spinal cord. The message is often not transmitted to your brain at all. Many reflex actions protect you from danger. Reflex movements are jerky because all the muscle fibers contract together to move the body away from danger as quickly as possible.

TEST YOUR REFLEXES

The "knee-jerk" reflex involves only one sensory and one motor neuron. Try it! Sit in a chair with one leg crossed loosely over the other. Get a friend to tap your crossed leg sharply just below the kneecap. What happens?

A sensory neuron in your skin responds to the pressure of the tap. It sends a message to your spinal cord. A message is carried back from your spinal cord by a motor neuron, telling your thigh muscle to contract. Your leg jerks upward as all the muscle fibers contract together. The path that the message takes is called the **reflex arc**. Doctors use this test to check that your reflexes are working well.

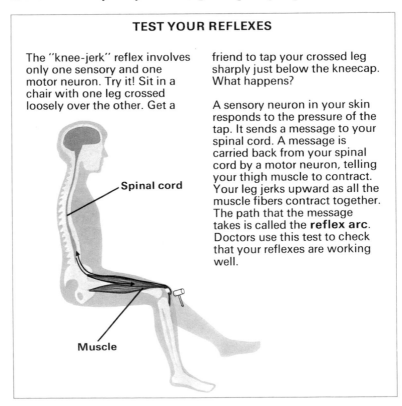

Spinal cord

Muscle

The Brain in Control

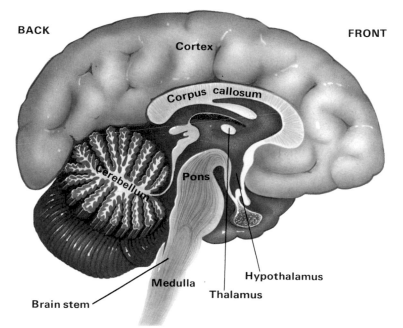

BACK / FRONT

Cortex

Corpus callosum

Cerebellum

Pons

Hypothalamus

Medulla

Thalamus

Brain stem

The brain is the body's control center. As well as keeping the body working smoothly, it is also responsible for your thoughts, feelings, and memory.

The brain needs a lot of energy to keep working efficiently. It uses one fifth of all the energy produced in your body. Because of this, the brain must have a constant supply of blood to provide it with the food and oxygen required to produce energy (see page 76). If there is not enough blood reaching your brain, you may faint. After about five minutes without oxygen, brain cells die. They can never be replaced.

Different parts of the brain have different jobs to do. The **medulla** controls involuntary activities – those we cannot consciously control – such as breathing and blood pressure. It is part of your autonomic nervous system. The **cerebellum** receives messages from your muscles and organs of balance and makes sure that your muscles work smoothly.

The largest area of the brain is the **cortex,** which controls all your conscious feelings and voluntary movements. It is also responsible for intelligence and learning. Certain parts of the cortex have specific jobs to do.

47

The Cortex

The cortex is the outer layer of the large, folded area of the brain called the **cerebrum.** The cerebrum is divided into two halves, also known as the left and right hemispheres. In each hemisphere, the cortex forms a layer of gray matter around an area of white matter. The two halves are linked together by bands of nerves, including those of the **corpus callosum** (see the diagram on page 47). The left-hand side of the cortex controls activities in the right-hand side of the body and the right-hand side controls those in the left. In right-handed people, the left half of the cortex directs speech, reading, and writing and the right half is responsible for their emotions and creativity. The opposite applies to left-handed people.

The cortex directs all your voluntary movements, receives messages from all your sense organs, and is responsible for your intelligence and personality. Different parts of the cortex are linked to different parts of the body. Sensations such as sight, hearing, smell, and taste are received by special (sensory) areas. Other (motor) areas send messages to certain parts of the body.

THE CORTEX

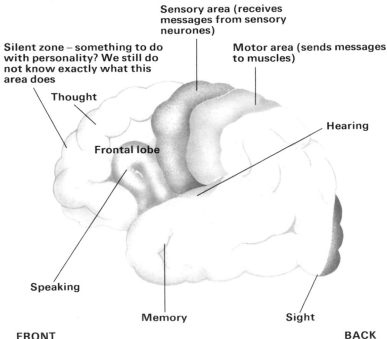

Sensory area (receives messages from sensory neurones)

Silent zone – something to do with personality? We still do not know exactly what this area does

Motor area (sends messages to muscles)

Thought

Hearing

Frontal lobe

Speaking

Memory

Sight

FRONT

BACK

48

BRAIN WAVES

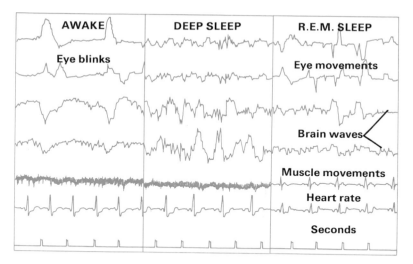

When You Sleep

When you are asleep, you become unconscious for a time and the cortex works far more slowly than when you are awake.

There are several kinds of sleep. When you are in the lightest phase of sleep, you often dream. This phase is called **R.E.M. (Rapid Eye Movement)** because during it, your eyes move backward and forward rapidly under closed eyelids. This usually happens just before you wake up. When you are most deeply asleep, growth hormones are released into your blood.

Sleep is important because it gives your body time to grow and repair itself. It also gives your brain time to sort out all of its experiences. There is still a lot that is not understood about sleep and dreaming.

▲ There is special equipment that can detect "brain waves" (electrical activity in the brain) and print them out as a pattern to show what is happening when people are awake and asleep. The equipment is called an **electroencephalograph** machine.

Outside Information

You have five senses – sight, hearing, smell, taste, and touch. Through these senses, your brain receives information about the world outside. A sense organ, for example the eye, contains many special receptor cells. These cells collect information and pass it to the sensory nerve cells which take it to the brain. Different receptors can receive information in the form of light rays, sound waves, chemicals, heat, or pressure.

Smell

Smell receptors are in the upper half of your nose, in a space called the **nasal cavity.** They cover an area about the same size as a postage stamp. The receptors are affected by scent particles (tiny chemical units called molecules) in the air. Each receptor cell has minute hairs which are covered with a sticky substance called **mucus.** Scent particles dissolve in the mucus and smell receptors send messages to the cortex of the brain via sensory neurons.

The brain can distinguish different smells. When you breathe normally, only a small number of scent molecules reach the smell receptors. If you want to identify a particular smell, you sniff. This carries more scent particles higher up your nostrils, onto the receptors.

Humans have a poor sense of smell when compared with other animals, but we can distinguish several thousand different smells. Some smells produce automatic responses. For example, the smell of food may automatically cause you to produce saliva or other digestive juices (because your body begins to expect food – see page 70), but unpleasant smells may make you feel unwell. You may lose your sense of smell for a short time when you have a cold because your nose is blocked and scent particles cannot reach the receptors.

▶ **A diagram of the inside** of the head, showing the nasal cavity and the mouth. The sensory cells that detect smells are found in the lining of the nose and those that detect tastes are found on the tongue.

ORGANS OF SMELL AND TASTE

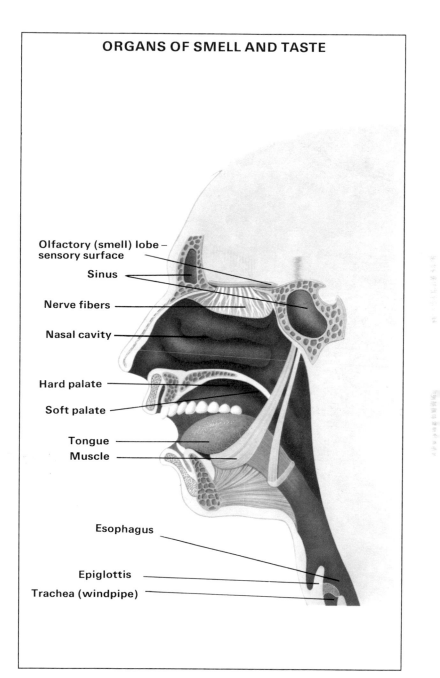

Olfactory (smell) lobe – sensory surface

Sinus

Nerve fibers

Nasal cavity

Hard palate

Soft palate

Tongue

Muscle

Esophagus

Epiglottis

Trachea (windpipe)

Taste

There are small groups of receptor cells in your tongue, called **taste buds.** Certain chemicals in food dissolve in the saliva in the mouth and stimulate these cells so that you can distinguish different tastes. Information about taste travels to the brain via sensory nerve cells and is dealt with by a special area of the cortex.

There are four basic tastes – bitter, sweet, sour, and salty. Different taste buds are sensitive to different kinds of taste. However, the various types of taste buds are not evenly distributed over your tongue. This means that some areas of the tongue are more sensitive to certain kinds of tastes than others.

Your senses of taste and smell work closely together. If you cannot smell properly, for example when you have a blocked nose because of a cold, you may also find that you cannot taste properly either.

THE TONGUE

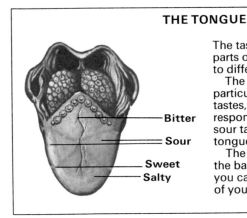

Bitter
Sour
Sweet
Salty

The taste buds on different parts of your tongue respond to different tastes.

The back of the tongue is particularly sensitive to bitter tastes, while the front and sides respond more to sweet and sour tastes. The middle of the tongue responds to salty tastes.

The taste buds are around the base of the tiny bumps that you can see all over the surface of your tongue.

DID YOU KNOW?

✳ With training, people can learn to distinguish many more tastes than is normal. Two examples of people who use this skill are tea and wine tasters.

✳ You also have taste buds on the root of your tongue and in the soft part of the back of the roof of your mouth.

✳ As people grow older, they have fewer taste buds and so become less sensitive to taste.

TEST YOUR SENSES

Taste and smell are two senses that depend a lot on each other. This means that information received from one sense can easily be confused by the workings of the other sense. You can test this out for yourself in the experiment on this page. You will need a friend to help you.

▶ 1. **Blindfold a friend** and ask him to taste two different foods with a similar shape and texture, for example a cube of uncooked potato and a cube of apple. Can he tell the difference?

Potato   **Apple**

▼ 2. **Try doing the same test** as in 1 but hold the taster's nose while he eats.

▼ 3. **Hold a piece of onion** under the taster's nose while he is eating a piece of apple. Ask him what he thinks he is eating.

Onion

53

Hearing and Balance

Your ears are not only sensitive to sounds but are also your organs of balance. The ear consists of three main areas: the **outer ear,** the **middle ear,** and the **inner ear.** Receptors for hearing and balance are found in your inner ear, which is deep inside your skull, behind and a little below your eyeball.

How Do We Hear Sounds?

Sounds are vibrations in the air. When a sound is made, the vibrations travel out in all directions. The outer part of your ear is specially shaped to collect these sound waves (even under water) and directs them down your ear canal to your eardrum or **tympanum**.

The eardrum is a very thin sheet of membrane stretched across the end of the canal. When sound waves hit it, it begins to vibrate like a drum and passes vibrations on to three small bones which form a bridge across your middle ear. These three bones are called the **hammer**, the **anvil,** and the **stirrup**, because of their shape. The last of the three bones, the stirrup, is connected to another membrane, called the **oval window**, which covers the entrance to the inner ear.

THE EAR

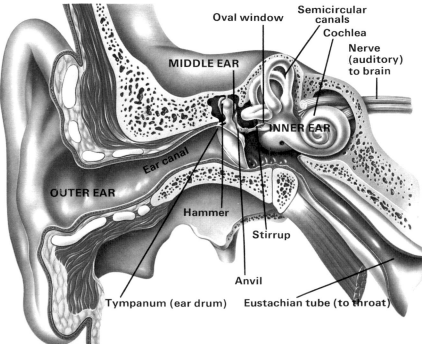

The oval window passes the vibrations on to the **cochlea**: a coiled tube that looks rather like a snail. It is filled with liquid and contains thousands of hair-like receptor cells. Some of these receptors are sensitive to low-pitched sounds and others to high-pitched ones. The receptors turn the vibrations into electrical messages which the brain can understand. From the cochlea in the inner ear, electrical impulses travel to the special part of the brain that deals with hearing. The brain is able to concentrate on the sounds that it wants to listen to and hold back the rest.

People can hear a wide range of sounds, from very high-pitched to very low-pitched. Listening to a full-sized orchestra gives a good idea of this range. Children have more sensitive ears than adults and are able to detect a wider variety of pitches.

WHICH DIRECTION?

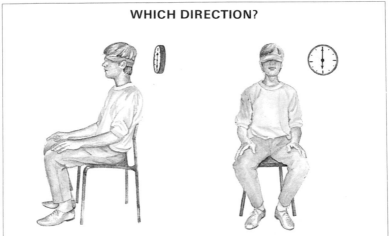

▲ 1. **Blindfold a friend** and position a ticking clock directly behind his head so that it is the **same** distance from both ears. Keeping the block behind your friend, try moving it to positions above and to the side of his head. Ask him to tell you each time where he thinks the clock is.

▲ 2. **Now try similar positions to the side** of your friend. How many times was he right? (Hint – try to stand in the same place each time you speak so that your voice does not provide any clues.)

If one ear receives sounds before the other, the brain can tell which direction the sounds are coming from. But if both ears receive sounds at the same time (when an object is the same distance from both of them), the direction from which sound is coming is much more difficult to work out.

Deafness

Loud noises cause the eardrum to tighten and the stirrup bone in the middle ear pulls away from the oval window in order to protect the ear. Spending long periods of time in loud noise makes the ear less sensitive and can cause deafness. People who work in noisy surroundings should wear ear muffs to protect their ears.

Deafness may also be caused by damage to the nerves which receive sounds, or by breaks in the eardrum (tympanum). Breaks in the eardrum can be caused by loud noises, sudden extreme changes in pressure, or infections. Small tears usually heal. Some types of deafness can be helped by hearing aids which work by making sounds louder.

Under Pressure

The **Eustacian tube** leads from the middle ear to the throat. When muscles allow this tube to open, air can get into, or out of, the middle ear. This makes sure the air pressure stays the same on either side of the eardrum.

If the air pressure changes quickly, for example when you are going up in an airplane, you may have to yawn or swallow in order to open your Eustacian tubes and balance the pressure in your ears. The popping sound you can often hear on these occasions is the Eustacian tubes opening. You may find that it helps to suck a candy just before an airplane takes off as this makes you swallow. Otherwise you might get discomfort in your ears from uneven pressure.

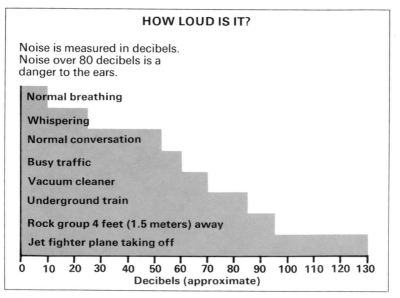

HOW LOUD IS IT?

Noise is measured in decibels. Noise over 80 decibels is a danger to the ears.

Normal breathing
Whispering
Normal conversation
Busy traffic
Vacuum cleaner
Underground train
Rock group 4 feet (1.5 meters) away
Jet fighter plane taking off

0 10 20 30 40 50 60 70 80 90 100 110 120 130
Decibels (approximate)

Balance and Position

The three **semicircular canals** near the cochlea in your inner ear give you your sense of balance. These three canals are at right angles to each other, rather like the back, base, and side of a cube.

The canals are filled with a fluid called **endolymph** and are lined with hair-like nerve endings. When you turn your head, the endolymph moves inside the canals and pushes on the nerve ends, which respond by sending messages to your brain. When you spin around and around, the endolymph moves so fast that it is still moving after you have stopped. This makes you feel dizzy for a short time.

Just below the semicircular canals are two small swellings, or sacs, called the **sacculus** and **utriculus.** Inside these there are sensory cells which have tiny hairs that are embedded in a kind of jelly. This jelly contains chalky particles called **otoliths.** If you tilt your head, these particles press on the hairs, causing the sensory cells to pass messages to your brain. In this way, you know your position in relation to the force of gravity. Even when you are under water with your eyes closed, you will always know which way is up.

As well as information from the semicircular canals, the brain also uses information it receives from your eyes, muscles, and joints to work out balance and position. Travel sickness is

▼ **The three semicircular canals** in the ear are arranged in a similar way to these three sides of a cube.

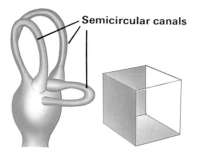

Semicircular canals

caused by your brain receiving two kinds of information that do not agree. Your ears and muscles tell the brain that you are not moving, while your eyes tell it that you are moving.

TEST YOUR BALANCE

Choose an object, close your eyes, and point to where you think it is. Open your eyes and check how accurate you were. Now spin around a couple of times and try to point to the object again.

The information your brain receives from the semicircular canals is confused by the spinning movement of the body and so it is difficult to be accurate, especially without any help from your eyes.

Ballet dancers keep their balance when spinning around fast by fixing their eyes on one point just before starting to spin and concentrating on it as they spin.

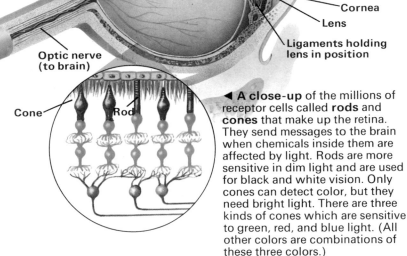

Bone of eye socket

Sclera (white of eye)

Retina

Optic nerve
(to brain)

Eyelid

Eyelashes

Conjunctiva

Iris

Pupil

Cornea

Lens

Ligaments holding
lens in position

Cone

Rod

◀ **A close-up** of the millions of receptor cells called **rods** and **cones** that make up the retina. They send messages to the brain when chemicals inside them are affected by light. Rods are more sensitive in dim light and are used for black and white vision. Only cones can detect color, but they need bright light. There are three kinds of cones which are sensitive to green, red, and blue light. (All other colors are combinations of these three colors.)

How You See

Perhaps the most important sense we have is our eyesight. Using our eyes we can move about easily, work, play, and recognize people. Our eyes receive information about the outside world as rays of light reflected from the objects we look at. Light rays enter the eyes through the pupil and are formed into a clear image (focused) onto the retina by the lens of the eye. Light receptor cells in the retina send messages to your brain in the form of electrical impulses.

The action of the eye is often compared to that of a camera. Both an eye and a camera are able to control the amount of light that enters and have a lens to focus the image onto a light-sensitive area.

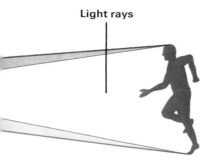

Light rays

◀ **Looking at objects.** When you look at something, light rays reflected from the object are bent as they pass through your cornea. The lens then focuses the rays so that an upside-down image of the object forms on your retina. Your brain interprets this image as being the right way up.

The Eye

The eyeball, a hollow sphere slightly smaller than a golf ball, has three main layers. A tough outer layer forms the white part of your eye. At the front of the eyeball this layer is transparent and is called the **cornea.** The middle layer of the eye is colored and at the front, where you can see it, it is called the **iris.** The layer which lines the inside of the eyeball is called the **retina.** Light-sensitive cells in the retina send messages to the brain via the **optic nerve.** The black dot that you can see in the center of the iris is the **pupil.** The **lens** is just behind the pupil and is protected by fluid in front and by clear jelly behind. This fluid and jelly also help to maintain the eyeball's shape. A thin, transparent membrane called the **conjunctiva** protects the front of your eye and lines your eyelids. Eyelids and lashes prevent large particles of dirt from reaching your eye, and tears (from special glands) wash the conjunctiva to keep it free from dust.

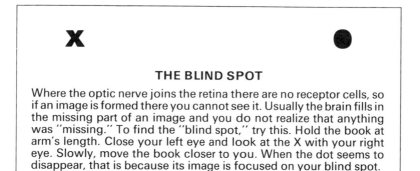

X   ●

THE BLIND SPOT

Where the optic nerve joins the retina there are no receptor cells, so if an image is formed there you cannot see it. Usually the brain fills in the missing part of an image and you do not realize that anything was "missing." To find the "blind spot," try this. Hold the book at arm's length. Close your left eye and look at the X with your right eye. Slowly, move the book closer to you. When the dot seems to disappear, that is because its image is focused on your blind spot.

NEAR AND FAR SIGHT

The process of bringing objects into focus is begun by the curved cornea and vital adjustments are made by the lens. Muscles holding the lens can contract, pulling the lens into a long, thin shape to focus distant objects, or relax, letting it go short and fat, to focus near objects. If the muscles are faulty, or the eyeball is the wrong shape, the image formed on the retina is not in focus. Below you can see ways in which naturally faulty sight can be corrected by wearing extra lenses – glasses or contact lenses.

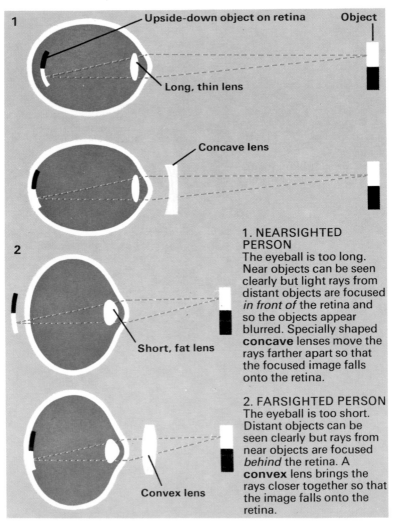

1

Upside-down object on retina

Object

Long, thin lens

Concave lens

2

Short, fat lens

Convex lens

1. NEARSIGHTED PERSON
The eyeball is too long. Near objects can be seen clearly but light rays from distant objects are focused *in front of* the retina and so the objects appear blurred. Specially shaped **concave** lenses move the rays farther apart so that the focused image falls onto the retina.

2. FARSIGHTED PERSON
The eyeball is too short. Distant objects can be seen clearly but rays from near objects are focused *behind* the retina. A **convex** lens brings the rays closer together so that the image falls onto the retina.

PROTECTING THE EYE FROM BRIGHT LIGHT

Your pupil is the hole in the center of the colored iris through which light enters the eye. Muscle around the pupil can contract to enlarge the pupil and relax to make it smaller. Try this experiment. In a dimly lit room, look at your pupils in a mirror. Now turn on a bright lamp and look again. In bright light, the pupils get smaller. This lets in less light and so protects the retina. Try the test again and this time notice how quickly the pupils change size. Then turn off the light and see how long it takes for the pupils to get larger again.

▲ **In bright light,** the pupil gets smaller to let in less light.

▲ **In dim light,** the pupil gets larger to let in more light.

IN THE THIRD DIMENSION....

Having two eyes enables you to judge distances more accurately. Close one eye and try to notice the difference. Each eye receives a slightly different view of an object and your brain combines the two views into one picture.

WHICH EYE?

To find out which eye you use more, try holding a pencil at arm's length, lined up with a distant object. Close one eye and then open it again. Repeat this with your other eye. The pencil will seem to jump sideways as either the right or the left eye closes. The eye that is closing when this happens is the one you use most – the **dominant** eye.

DID YOU KNOW?

✳ The tendency to see certain colors abnormally – color-blindness – is probably caused by faulty cones. About 8 percent of males are affected, but few females are. Most color-blind people suffer from red-green color-blindness, which means that they cannot see these two colors correctly.

✳ Vitamin A is needed to make the light-sensitive chemical inside rods and cones. This vitamin is found in carrots.

Touch

If you close your eyes and block your ears and nose, you can still discover a lot about the world around you from your sense of touch. Because you need to be near to things to touch them, blind people use sticks to extend their range. People who cannot see use their sense of touch to "read" books specially made in braille – patterns of raised bumps representing letters and words.

The receptors in your skin are not only sensitive to things touching them. In fact, there are several different kinds of receptors, enabling you to feel temperature, texture, pressure, and pain. There are more receptors for pain than for the other categories. Pain warns us that something is wrong, for example when we step on a pin or touch something hot.

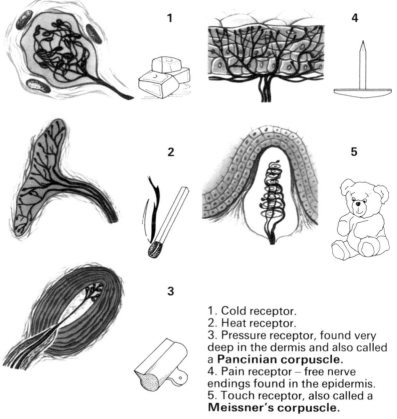

1. Cold receptor.
2. Heat receptor.
3. Pressure receptor, found very deep in the dermis and also called a **Pancinian corpuscle.**
4. Pain receptor – free nerve endings found in the epidermis.
5. Touch receptor, also called a **Meissner's corpuscle.**

HOW SENSITIVE ARE YOU?

EXPERIMENT 1. Test your temperature sensitivity by filling one cup with hot, one with cold, and one with warm water. Put the first finger of the left hand in the hot water and the same finger of your right hand in the cold water for about one minute. Now, dip each of the two fingers alternately in and out of the warm water. The finger from the hot water will feel cold, but the finger from the cold water will feel warm. This shows how receptors in the skin respond to changes in temperature. One finger signals a drop in temperature, while the other signals an increase.

EXPERIMENT 2. Some parts of the skin are more sensitive than others because they have more receptor cells. You can test this out for yourself. Press two pins into a cork so that the heads are about $\frac{1}{2}$ inch (1·5cm) apart. Ask a friend to close her eyes, then touch her on the back of the neck, the back of the hand, and the fingertips with the two pinheads. Ask her each time how many points she can feel. In very sensitive areas, such as the fingertips and tongue, she will be able to distinguish two points, but in less sensitive areas she will only feel one. (Hint – use just one point on some occasions, so that your friend does not expect two.)

▼ **Experiment 1**   ▼ **Experiment 2**

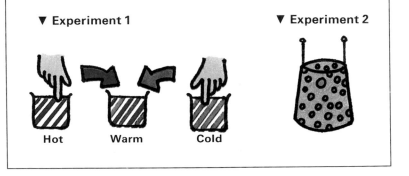

Hot   Warm   Cold

Three blind men examined an elephant. The first man felt the elephant's legs. "An elephant has four pillars like tree trunks," he said. The second man, on examining the elephant's trunk, said: "An elephant is long and flexible, like a snake." The third man just stood near the elephant feeling the breeze from its ears and declared: "The elephant is like a big fan."

This story shows that although we may all experience the same things, we all interpret them in different ways and our senses work together to give us a more complete picture of what is happening.

How a Body Keeps Going

In some ways, your body is like a car. Both need certain things to keep them running smoothly. Of course your body is far more complicated than a machine because it can do most things automatically, by itself.

The human body is like a very complicated piece of engineering. Just as a car cannot work without **fuel**, the body gets the energy it needs to drive itself from another kind of fuel – a well-balanced diet. Both cars and humans need to get rid of their **waste,** and of course **maintenance** and **repair** is required to keep any machine in good working order.

YLX 542

65

Supplying the Fuel

The things that you eat and drink make up your diet. They provide you with the energy needed to keep the body working and the nourishing substances – **nutrients** – which are vital for growth and repair.

Different types of food contain different nutrients which are used for particular jobs in your body. The amount of certain nutrients that you need varies slightly as you grow older, but basically everybody needs a good balance of each type. Your diet must include **proteins**, **carbohydrates**, **fats**, **mineral salts**, **vitamins,** and **water**.

PROTEINS

More than 10 percent of your body tissue is made of protein – a body-building substance found in foods such as fish, meat, cheese, nuts, eggs, and milk. You need proteins so that you can grow and also to repair and replace damaged cells.

Proteins consist of units called **amino acids** that are joined together. When protein that you have eaten is processed by your digestive system (see page 70), amino acids are separated from each other. These amino acids travel in your blood to your cells, where they are reassembled into the particular proteins that you need. If you eat more protein than your body needs, the extra amount is broken down by your liver.

The difference between one protein and another depends on the number and type of amino acids that they contain. There are millions of different kinds of protein, but only 20 different kinds of amino acid. To stay healthy, we need all 20 kinds. Eggs, milk, and most meats contain all 20 amino acids, but some beans and nuts do not.

▶ **Some of the foods** that contain protein.

► **Common foods** that supply us with carbohydrates.

CARBOHYDRATES

Carbohydrates in our food supply us with energy (see page 76). The main types of carbohydrates are sugars and a substance called **starch**. Bread and potatoes contain starch, table sugar is a sugar called sucrose, and fruit and jam contain a sugar called **glucose**. Only glucose can be used by the body for energy, so all other forms of carbohydrates have to be broken down and turned into glucose inside the body by the digestive process.

The amount of energy which can be produced from different foods is measured in Calories. A glass of milk contains 150 Calories while a boiled egg has 80 Calories. The number of Calories a person needs each day depends on how active he is. For example, swimming uses up about 600 Calories an hour, but sleeping uses only 70 Calories an hour. On average, a man needs about 3,000 Calories each day, a woman needs around 2,200 Calories, and a child of 4 years old needs about 1,600.

If you eat more carbohydrates than your body needs, the extra amount is stored as fat. The body can convert this fat store into energy if it has to, but eating too much carbohydrates over a long period of time can make you put on weight. This can put a strain on your heart and is a common cause of heart disease.

MINERAL SALTS

Small amounts of chemicals called minerals are vital for the smooth running of your body. **Calcium** and **phosphorus** – found in milk and cheese – help to build healthy bones and teeth. Your red blood cells need **iron**, from foods such as meat, liver, and spinach. **Sodium** and **potassium** are needed by your nerves. We can get sodium from **sodium chloride** – table salt. Small amounts of **fluoride** help to prevent tooth decay and **iodine** – found in fish – is essential for growth.

FATS

Fats are used in your body to form cell parts and for energy production. Fat stored under the skin provides a store of energy and a layer of insulation. It is harder to digest than carbohydrates but produces twice as much energy as the same amount of carbohydrates. About 25 percent of your energy comes from the fats you eat.

► **Fat is found** in foods such as milk, vegetable oil, butter, and meat fat.

VITAMINS

You need small amounts of 15 different vitamins to keep the chemical processes in your body going. Your body cannot make any vitamins except vitamin D, so you must eat foods which contain them in order to stay healthy.

VITAMIN	FOUND IN . . .	NEEDED FOR . . .
A	Milk, butter, eggs, green vegetables, fish oil, liver (and carotene in carrots)	Fighting disease and seeing in the dark
B₁ (thiamine)	Yeast and wheat germ (whole wheat bread)	All "B" vitamins needed for healthy appetite, energy production in cells, and healthy nerves and skin
B₂	Yeast	
9 other "B" vitamins	Milk, meat, and green vegetables	
C	Oranges, lemons, tomatoes, black currants, strawberries, and fresh vegetables	Healthy blood and gums, healing wounds, and possibly protection against colds
D	Cod-liver oil, cream, egg yolks (and with sunlight, fat below the skin forms vitamin D)	Strong bones and teeth
E	Whole wheat bread, brown rice, and butter	Not fully understood
K	Green vegetables, liver	Clotting blood

WATER

About 70 percent of your body is made of water. Although you might be able to live for 2 to 3 weeks without food, without water, you could die in 2 or 3 days. An adult loses about half a gallon (2 to 3 liters) every day in sweat, urine, and through breathing. About half of this is replaced by drinking, and the rest comes from foods – for example, melon, summer squash, and lettuce are about 90 percent water.

COOKING FOOD

Cooking makes food easier to chew and digest and makes many foods look and taste better. High temperatures kill many bacteria in food and so make it safe to eat. However, if green vegetables are overcooked, more than 50 percent of the vitamin C they contain can be destroyed.

FIBER

Fiber (roughage) is the part of your food which cannot be broken down and passes out of your body. It comes from fruit, vegetables, and whole wheat bread. Because it is bulky, it helps the colon muscles to work properly and so prevents you from becoming constipated.

Fiber is an essential part of a healthy diet.

MILK

Milk is the only food a baby needs for its first few months. Mother's milk contains all the protein, carbohydrate, minerals, and vitamins that a baby needs, but it does not contain much iron. Babies have stores of iron in their bodies, but as these get used up and they begin to need more of other nutrients, they must start eating solid foods.

MEDICAL FACTS

● Cholesterol is a type of fat found, for example, in eggs and shellfish. Too much of it can increase the risk of a heart attack.

● People in the richer countries of the world tend to eat too much table salt, which may lead to high blood pressure.

● If you do not eat enough iron, you can suffer from **anemia**, which makes you tired and listless.

● Children need about 3 or 4 grams of protein for every kilogram (about 2 pounds) of their body's weight because they are growing. Teenagers need even more than this.

What Happens to Food?

Before nutrients from food can be absorbed into the bloodstream and used by the body's cells, the food has to be chopped up and broken down. This is what your digestive system does. The digestive system is a long tube that begins at your mouth and ends at your anus. In an adult it is up to $29\frac{1}{2}$ feet (9 meters) long.

Digestion starts with your first bite. In your mouth, food is chopped up and mixed with **saliva**, a digestive juice which begins breaking carbohydrates down into glucose. Your tongue rolls the food into a ball, which is pushed into your food pipe – the **esophagus** – and moved down to your stomach by a process called **peristalsis** (see diagram below). When you swallow food, a "lid" – the **epiglottis** – usually comes right down over your windpipe so that food does not go down there instead of down your esophagus.

Food stays in your stomach for about 3 hours. Here it is mixed with more digestive juices containing **enzymes** and **acid**, which are produced in the walls of the stomach. Enzymes are special proteins that work throughout your body to speed up the chemical changes that are constantly taking place. Digestive juices contain several different enzymes that help to break down food. The acid in your stomach allows the enzymes to work and helps to kill any bacteria in the food.

By this stage the food is like a creamy soup. It leaves your stomach a little at a time and goes into your **small intestine**. This is the longest part of the digestive system – up to 13 feet (4 meters) long – and is neatly coiled in your abdomen. In the first part of the small intestine – the **duodenum** – digestive juices from the **pancreas**, **gall bladder**, and small intestine walls are added. Food gradually moves along, being digested (broken down) as it goes, until it reaches the last part of the small intestine – the **ileum** – from where it is absorbed into your blood.

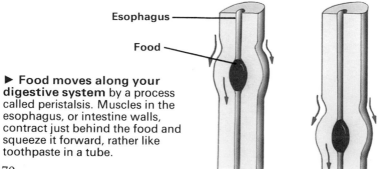

Esophagus

Food

► **Food moves along your digestive system** by a process called peristalsis. Muscles in the esophagus, or intestine walls, contract just behind the food and squeeze it forward, rather like toothpaste in a tube.

THE DIGESTIVE SYSTEM

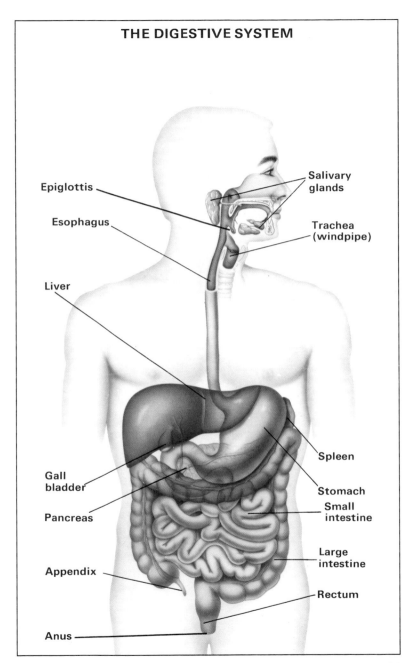

Epiglottis

Salivary glands

Esophagus

Trachea (windpipe)

Liver

Spleen

Gall bladder

Stomach

Pancreas

Small intestine

Appendix

Large intestine

Rectum

Anus

Absorbing Food

The lining of the small intestine is folded into millions of tiny fingers or **villi** (just one is a **villus**). Each villus contains a network of blood vessels and a lymph vessel (see page 94). Amino acids and glucose pass through the villus into the bloodstream and digested fats go into the lymph vessel. Undigested food continues on to the first part of your **large intestine** – the **colon**. Here, some of the water passes into the bloodstream through the colon walls. The mostly solid waste matter now left in the colon travels on to the last part of your intestine –

the **rectum**. It is stored for a while in the rectum before leaving your body as **feces** through your **anus** when you go to the toilet.

The Liver

The liver is the body's largest organ and one of the most important. Most digested food goes to the liver before traveling to the rest of the body. The liver processes amino acids and stores vitamins. It also stores a substance called **glycogen**. When there is a good supply of glucose, the liver converts it into gly-

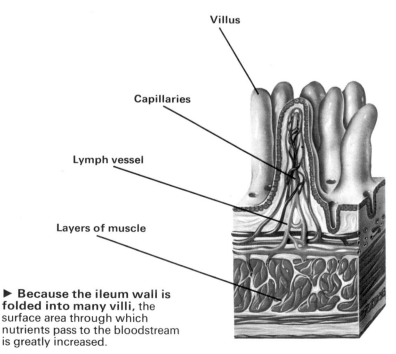

Villus

Capillaries

Lymph vessel

Layers of muscle

▶ **Because the ileum wall is folded into many villi,** the surface area through which nutrients pass to the bloodstream is greatly increased.

cogen, which can be turned back into glucose and used anywhere in the body when needed. A substance called **insulin** (a hormone from the pancreas) switches on the conversion of glucose to glycogen. Without insulin too much glucose stays in the blood and can lead to an illness called diabetes (see page 90). The liver also produces a substance called **bile**, which helps in the digestion of fats in the duodenum. Bile is stored in the gall bladder until it is needed.

As a result of the many chemical reactions that take place in the liver, a lot of heat is produced there. The inside of the body is kept warm by the blood being heated up as it passes through the liver. The liver also helps to break up old red blood cells when they wear out after a few months. Any hemoglobin which is not needed is eventually turned into a brown substance which gives feces their color.

Chemical reactions in our bodies often produce poisonous, or **toxic**, substances. Also, some of the food that we eat may have toxic contents. The liver turns these toxic substances into harmless ones. This process is called **detoxication**.

MEDICAL FACTS

● The **appendix** is a dead-ending tube at the junction of the small and large intestines. It is not used in human digestion but is important in animals that eat grass. Sometimes people get **appendicitis**. This is caused by the appendix becoming infected and inflamed. It then has to be removed.

● **Indigestion** is a pain in the stomach which some people feel after eating. It may be caused by eating too fast or by the stomach producing too much acid. People who worry a lot tend to produce a lot of acid in their stomach. Some of this may rise up in their throat and cause a burning feeling. This acid may also damage the lining of the stomach and lead to stomach **ulcers**.

● **Vomiting** can be caused by eating food which is bad or just by eating too much. The muscles of your diaphragm and abdomen walls contract and force the unwanted contents of your stomach back up and out of your body.

● **Diarrhea** may be caused by food poisoning or by an infection in your intestines. The result is that food travels rapidly through the digestive system and water is not absorbed from it in the colon. You may feel very thirsty and should drink a lot to make up for the water you are losing.

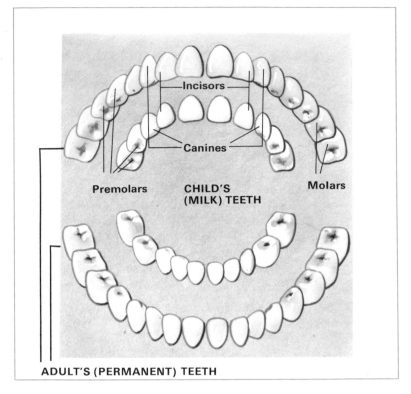

Incisors

Canines

Premolars   CHILD'S
(MILK) TEETH

Molars

ADULT'S (PERMANENT) TEETH

Teeth

Before our food is broken down chemically and absorbed, it must first be chopped into small bits that are easier to digest. This is what your **teeth** do and so they are really the first part of the digestive system.

At the front of your mouth you have sharp **incisor** teeth that cut and chop food. Beside these are the **canine** teeth – also used for cutting and for tearing. Farther around, at the sides of your mouth, are the **premolar** teeth. Right at the back of your mouth are **molars**. The premolar and molar teeth have large, uneven top surfaces which are ideal for grinding food.

A baby is usually born without teeth. By the time it is two years old it will have grown 20 "milk" teeth. At about 6 years old, a child begins to grow adult teeth, which push out and replace the milk teeth. A full set of adult teeth numbers 32, but some adults never grow their four back molar – **wisdom** – teeth.

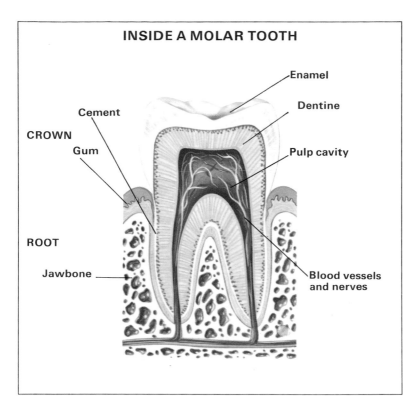

INSIDE A MOLAR TOOTH

Enamel

Dentine

Cement

CROWN

Gum

Pulp cavity

ROOT

Jawbone

Blood vessels and nerves

The outer layer of your teeth is made of **enamel**. This is the hardest substance in the body and provides a tough biting or grinding surface. Under the enamel is a layer of **dentine** – a substance which is rather like bone. Inside the dentine there is an area called the **pulp cavity**. This cavity contains blood vessels and nerves, which make the tooth sensitive to pain and temperature. The part of the tooth that you can see above the gum is called the **crown**. Below the gum is the **root** of the tooth. The root is held in place in the jawbone by a layer of bone tissue called **cement**.

What Can Go Wrong?
Bacteria in our mouths feed on the sugar in any food particles left between our teeth and produce acid. The saliva can get rid of some of this acid, but not before it starts to damage the enamel. Sticky food and bacteria form a thin layer over our teeth called **plaque**. We get tooth decay if we allow too much plaque to build up by eating too many sugary foods and by not brushing our teeth regularly.

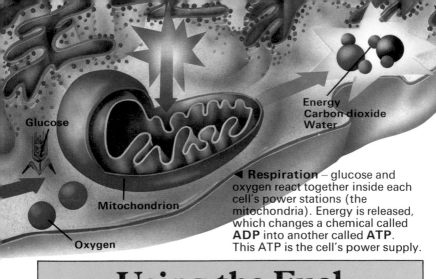

Glucose

Mitochondrion

Oxygen

Energy
Carbon dioxide
Water

◀ **Respiration** – glucose and oxygen react together inside each cell's power stations (the mitochondria). Energy is released, which changes a chemical called **ADP** into another called **ATP**. This ATP is the cell's power supply.

Using the Fuel

Your body uses energy to keep going and to grow. In order to get energy from the food you eat, your body has first to combine that food with oxygen – a gas found in the air. When you breathe in, oxygen goes into your lungs and your blood carries it from there to all the cells in your body. Inside each cell, the oxygen combines with glucose from food and as a result, energy is released. This process is called **respiration**. Two waste products are also produced during this process – a gas called **carbon dioxide**, and **water**. These are taken back to the lungs to leave the body when you breathe out.

Breathing

When you breathe in, air is sucked in through your nose or mouth and goes down your **trachea** (windpipe). Your trachea branches into two main **bronchi**. One **bronchus** goes to the left lung and the other to the right lung. These bronchi divide into smaller and smaller bronchi, the smallest of which are called **bronchioles**. The smallest bronchioles are only $\frac{1}{50}$ inch across and each one ends in a bunch of tiny air sacs called **alveoli** (one is an **alveolus**). From the alveoli, oxygen passes into the bloodstream. The hundreds of millions of alveoli make the overall surface area of the lungs very large, so that a maximum amount of oxygen can be passed to the blood. The oxygen travels in the blood to each cell in the body where it is used for respiration.

THE RESPIRATORY SYSTEM

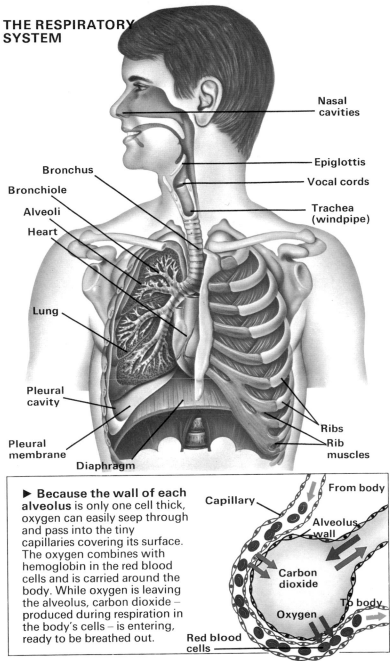

Nasal cavities

Epiglottis

Vocal cords

Trachea (windpipe)

Bronchus

Bronchiole

Alveoli

Heart

Lung

Pleural cavity

Pleural membrane

Diaphragm

Ribs

Rib muscles

▶ **Because the wall of each alveolus** is only one cell thick, oxygen can easily seep through and pass into the tiny capillaries covering its surface. The oxygen combines with hemoglobin in the red blood cells and is carried around the body. While oxygen is leaving the alveolus, carbon dioxide – produced during respiration in the body's cells – is entering, ready to be breathed out.

From body

Capillary

Alveolus wall

Carbon dioxide

To body

Oxygen

Red blood cells

How You Breathe

Your lungs have no muscles of their own. It is the muscles in your chest that control breathing. The **diaphragm** is a sheet of muscle tissue which forms the floor of your chest. There are other muscles between your ribs which can contract to move your ribs.

You breathe in when the diaphragm contracts and moves down. The rib muscles contract and the ribs move up and out. This increases the space inside your chest. The lungs themselves are in their own airtight space called the **pleural cavity**. When the space inside the chest increases, the air pressure in the lungs is less than the air pressure outside the body. Air rushes into the lungs to make the pressure equal. You breathe out when the diaphragm relaxes and moves up. The muscles between the ribs relax so that the ribs move down and in. The space in the chest is decreased and so air pressure in the lungs is greater than outside the body. Air rushes out to make the pressure equal.

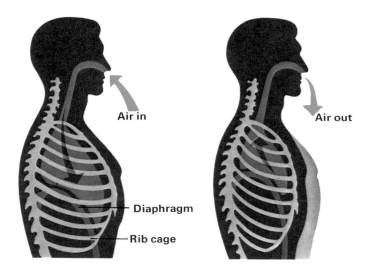

1. Breathing in.
Diaphragm contracts and moves down. Rib muscles contract and ribs move up and out. The space inside the chest has increased so pressure is greater outside than inside the lungs. Air is breathed in to make the pressure equal.

2. Breathing out.
Diaphragm relaxes and arches upward. Rib muscles relax and ribs move down and in. The space inside the chest has decreased so pressure inside the lungs is greater than outside the body. Air rushes out to make the air pressure equal.

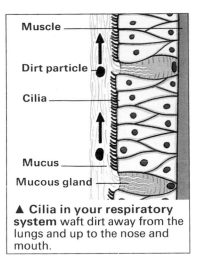

▲ **Cilia in your respiratory system** waft dirt away from the lungs and up to the nose and mouth.

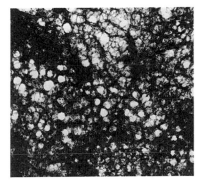

▲ **This microscope slide** of lung tissue shows how the cells can become clogged by harmful substances.

Protecting the Lungs

The air that you breathe in may be too cold or hot, too dirty or too dry. To protect the lungs, air is warmed and filtered. Dry air is moistened inside the nose and cold air is heated by the blood vessels in the nasal cavity. Your nose also contains hairs which trap large particles of dust and dirt. Smaller particles are trapped by sticky mucus in your nose, throat, and air passages. Tiny, hair-like **cilia** waft the mucus which contains these particles away from your lungs and back up to your nose or mouth to be sneezed or blown out, or swallowed. When you have a cold, more mucus is produced. Coughing forces a gust of air up from the lungs and carries with it harmful particles which irritate the lining of the bronchi, trachea, or throat.

Smoking and Pollution

A new baby's lungs are pink, but over the years lungs get blackened from breathing in dirty and polluted air. Dirt clogs the alveoli and air passages and makes the lungs less efficient.

People who smoke are especially likely to develop diseases of the respiratory system. Tobacco contains dangerous chemicals and a harmful substance called nicotine. These irritate the air passages and make the cilia in them less able to clear away mucus and the particles mucus contains. Mucus and dirt build up in smokers' lungs and the cough that they develop is caused by their lungs trying to clear away the mucus. Smoking is one of the main causes of lung cancer and bronchitis. Many people die each year from lung cancer caused by smoking.

FIND YOUR LUNG VOLUME

▶ 1. **Mark a large plastic bottle** at 1 pint (half liter) intervals by pouring into it one pint of water at a time from a measuring jug, up to almost a gallon (4 liters). Add more water until the bottle is full.

Ordinary kitchen measuring jug

Plastic tubing

Kitchen sink or basin

▲ 2. **Turn the bottle upside down** in a basin of water, making sure that none escapes. Put a tube through the opening of the bottle. Now, supporting the bottle with one or both hands, take a deep breath and blow hard down the tube. Your breath will collect in the bottle and force out some of the water. You can now check the water level to find the volume (capacity) of your lungs.

Try breathing as normally as possible, in and out, down the tube. Notice the volume exchanged during this "quiet" breathing.

Talking

The **"voice box"** – also called the **larynx** – is at the upper end of your trachea. The larynx shows up on the outside of your throat as your **Adam's apple**. Two bands of cartilage are stretched across the opening into the larynx. These are called your **vocal cords**. Sounds are made when air is forced through the vocal cords, making them vibrate. The muscles of the larynx are able to alter the shape of the cords to produce low-pitched or high-pitched sounds. You use the muscles of your throat, mouth, and lips to form the sounds into words.

The harder you breathe out, the louder the sounds that you make. To test this, see how long you can talk without taking a breath. Now try again, this time shouting without stopping for a breath. Because you use more breath for shouting, you cannot keep it up for so long.

1

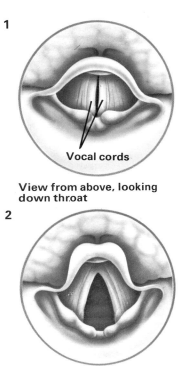

View from above, looking down throat

2

► **Your vocal cords** produce high-pitched sounds when they are close together (diagram 1) and low-pitched sounds when far apart (diagram 2).

DID YOU KNOW?

✳ Adults' lungs hold about 5 pints (3 liters) of air. In quiet breathing the diaphragm moves up and down less than $\frac{1}{2}$ inch (about 10mm) and about 1 pint ($\frac{1}{2}$ liter) of air is breathed in and out, roughly 15 times every minute. During vigorous exercise, the breathing rate increases and breathing is much deeper, because the diaphragm can move as much as 2 inches (60mm).

✳ The area of your lungs is 753 square feet (70 square meters), about 40 times greater than the area covered by your skin. This is because of the enormous number of tiny alveoli and means that you can take in the amount of air that you need.

✳ **Hiccoughs** are caused by your diaphragm contracting so quickly that you take a short gasp of air. The sound that you hear is your vocal cords closing suddenly.

What About Waste?

The waste left over from food that you do not digest leaves your body as feces. But your body produces other waste substances that it must get rid of. These include the carbon dioxide and water made during respiration and a substance called **urea**. Urea is made by the liver from amino acids (see page 66) that are left over after the body has used what it needs. Urea leaves your body in sweat and **urine**. Urine is a liquid made up mainly of water and urea and is produced in the kidneys.

Controlling Water

The level of water in your body must be regulated and distributed evenly. You take water in when you eat and drink and lose some through breathing and sweating. You may lose $2-3\frac{1}{2}$ pints (1–2 liters) of water a day just through breathing.

The Kidneys

The amount of water in your body is controlled mainly by how much urine your kidneys produce. If you drink a lot, a lot of urine is produced, because the body does not need most of the water. If you drink less, or lose a lot of water in other ways, such as sweating, the kidneys produce less urine. As well as water and urea, the kidneys help to control the level of salts in your body.

Your kidneys are just below the lowest ribs in your back. Each one is about 5 by 2 inches (110mm long and 50mm wide) and receives blood from a **renal** artery. Urine produced in the kidneys runs down two thin tubes called **ureters**, which lead to your **bladder**. Urine leaves your body through the **urethra**. In males the urethra is longer than in females because it extends to the tip of the penis.

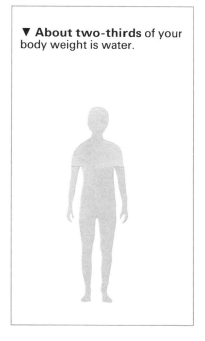

▼ **About two-thirds** of your body weight is water.

THE EXCRETORY SYSTEM

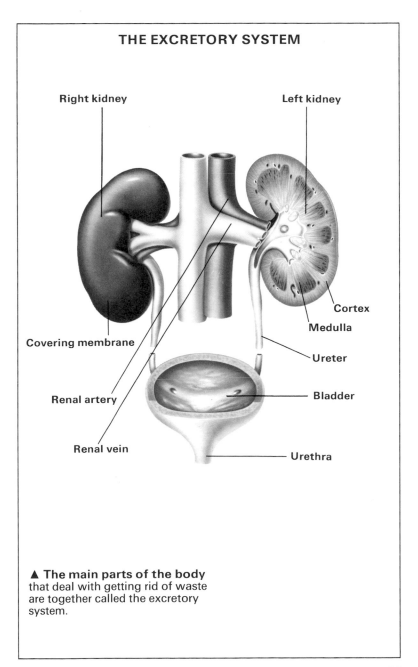

Right kidney

Left kidney

Cortex

Medulla

Covering membrane

Ureter

Renal artery

Bladder

Renal vein

Urethra

▲ **The main parts of the body** that deal with getting rid of waste are together called the excretory system.

A KIDNEY TUBULE

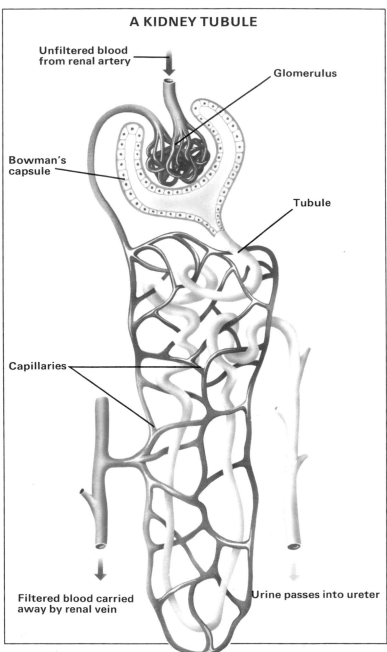

Unfiltered blood from renal artery

Glomerulus

Bowman's capsule

Tubule

Capillaries

Filtered blood carried away by renal vein

Urine passes into ureter

How Your Kidneys Work

Your kidneys are really a pair of highly efficient filters. The millions of tiny filtering units inside them are called **nephrons**. Each nephron consists of a cup-shaped structure – a **Bowman's capsule** – with a winding tube coming from it. Nephrons filter about 33 gallons (150 liters) of fluid each day.

The renal arteries that provide the kidneys with their blood supply divide into many tiny branches. Every tiny branch in turn ends in a bunch of capillaries that is called a **glomerulus**. A glomerulus is always surrounded by the Bowman's capsule of a nephron. Blood in the glomerulus is under high pressure, which forces part of the plasma – containing water, amino acids, glucose, salts, and urea – through the capillary walls and into the capsule. The red and white cells, proteins, and platelets in the blood are too large to pass through.

The filtered liquid goes on into the nephron tubule, which is itself surrounded by a network of capillaries. Regulated amounts of substances which the body still needs pass through the tubule walls and back into the bloodstream. These substances include salts, amino acids, and most of the water. The liquid which remains inside the tubule is urine and 96 percent of it is water. The urine continues down the tubule, which joins up with other nephron tubules to form the ureter. The ureter takes the urine into the bladder – a muscular bag which can store up to $\frac{3}{4}$ of a pint (400cc) of liquid. A muscle around the exit from the bladder – the **sphincter** – keeps urine inside. When this muscle relaxes, the urine flows out of the body.

▼ An X ray photograph, showing the kidneys and spinal cord. Notice that the right kidney (left of picture) is lower than the other.

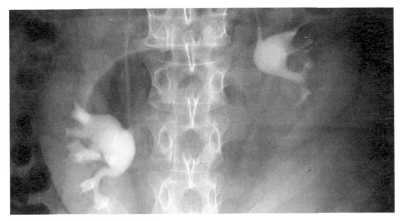

Kidney Machines

Your kidneys may stop working or be inefficient for a while as a result of an accident or disease. If this happens, a special machine can be used to filter your blood for you. This artificial filtering process is called **dialysis**. The way it works is that your blood is led into the machine through a tube connected to an artery in your arm. Inside the machine, the blood is pumped through cellophane tubing. This tubing is coiled in a container of liquid that has been warmed to body temperature. The liquid contains specific amounts of salts and sugars. Waste substances in the blood pass through the cellophane and into this liquid, so that the blood is "cleaned." Substances needed by the blood pass into it from the liquid. The clean blood is then returned to your body. It re-enters the arm through a vein to which a tube is attached.

Blood must pass through the machine 20 times before it is cleaned properly. People who need dialysis treatment must spend two twelve-hour sessions connected to the machine every week. They must also follow special diets.

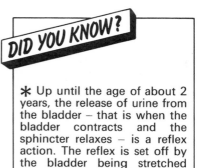

DID YOU KNOW?

✳ Up until the age of about 2 years, the release of urine from the bladder – that is when the bladder contracts and the sphincter relaxes – is a reflex action. The reflex is set off by the bladder being stretched when it is full. After this age, the action can be controlled voluntarily.

KIDNEY TRANSPLANTS

Because a person can survive with only one kidney, it is possible to donate a kidney to someone else. You could not survive for very long without any kidneys because the imbalance of salts in your blood would lead to heart failure. Some people choose to carry special Donor Cards which say that if they die they would like their kidneys to be donated to someone in need. It is vital that any donated kidney should match the tissue type of the person to whom it is being given, otherwise it could be rejected. This applies also to any other type of transplant.

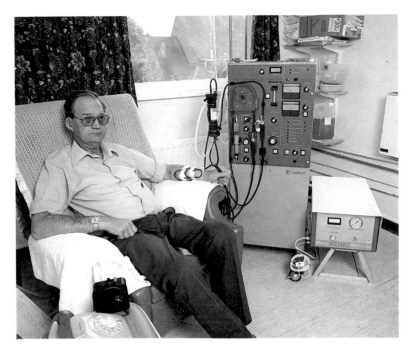

▼ **This diagram** shows the route taken by blood undergoing the artificial filtering process that is called dialysis.

▲ Not all patients who need dialysis treatment have to go to the hospital. Some have machines that they can use at home.

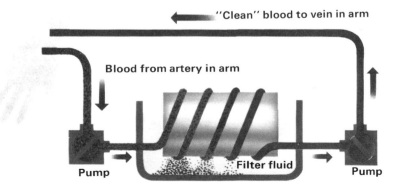

⟵ "Clean" blood to vein in arm

Blood from artery in arm

Pump

Filter fluid

Pump

THE ENDOCRINE (HORMONE) SYSTEM

For easy reference, both male
and female glands have been
put on one diagram

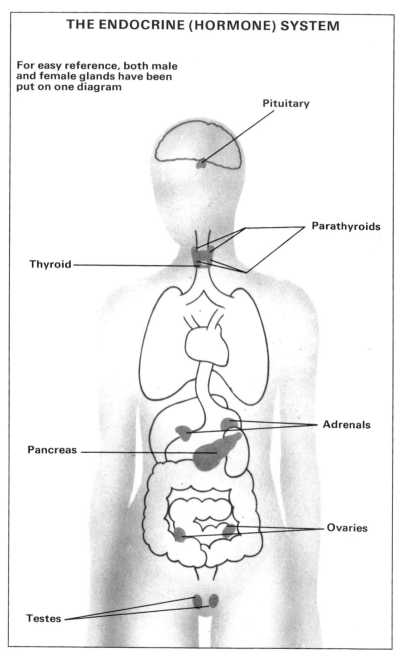

Pituitary

Parathyroids

Thyroid

Adrenals

Pancreas

Ovaries

Testes

Fine Tuning

There are special groups of cells in your body called **endocrine glands**. These glands produce chemical substances called **hormones**. Hormones are carried around the body in the bloodstream to control and adjust certain processes. Most hormones work over a long period of time. Some work on a particular organ, while others affect the whole body.

The "Master Gland"

One of the most important endocrine glands is the **pituitary**. This is a small gland attached to the underside of your brain. It produces several hormones, some of which control other endocrine glands. This is why it is often called the master gland. The pituitary is linked to the hypothalamus region of the brain. This region helps to control the pituitary. It also controls hunger, thirst, and sleep.

One of the hormones that the pituitary produces is often called **growth** hormone. This controls your rate of growth by regulating the amounts of nutrients taken into your cells. Another hormone released by the pituitary is **ADH** (**a**ntidiuretic **h**ormone). ADH helps to keep your water balance correct by controlling the amount of urine that your kidneys produce.

Oxytocin is a hormone from the pituitary that stimulates the contractions of the uterus when a baby is being born. The hormone which controls milk production in a woman ready for breastfeeding a baby is called **prolactin** and also comes from the pituitary gland.

The Thyroid Gland

The hormone **thyroxine** is produced by your thyroid gland. This gland is found in your neck, in front of your windpipe. Thyroxine controls the rate at which food is converted to energy (by respiration, see page 76) in your cells. Too much thyroxine can make people very thin and over-active (or **hyperactive**). Too little and they may be very slow and overweight.

There are other tiny glands which are behind your thyroid and are called the **parathyroid** glands. They produce a hormone which regulates the amount of calcium in your bones and blood.

The Ovaries

The ovaries – part of the female reproductive system – produce two hormones called **estrogen** and **progesterone**. These prepare the uterus for pregnancy and control the woman's female characteristics. (The ovaries also produce a woman's ova cells.)

The Testes

The part of the male reproductive system called the testes produces a hormone called **testosterone**. This controls the production of sperm cells and also a man's masculine appearance.

The Pancreas

The pancreas produces a hormone called **insulin**. This controls the level of glucose in your blood. It also regulates the conversion of any excess glucose to stored glycogen. The level of glucose in your blood is kept at between 0.002 and 0.005 oz. in every 6 in.^{3} (80 and 150 mg in every 100 cm^3) of blood. After a meal, the glucose level rises as you digest your food and carbohydrates are broken down into glucose. When this happens, insulin is released from the pancreas. Insulin causes some of the glucose to be changed into glycogen. This glycogen is stored in your liver and muscles for future use. A

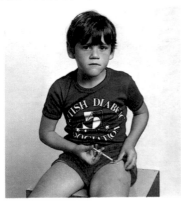

▲ **A diabetic boy** giving himself an injection of insulin.

healthy adult has about $3\frac{1}{2}$ oz. (100 g) of glycogen stored in his or her body.

As the level of glucose in your blood falls in the hours after a meal, less insulin is released. If the level of glucose falls to less than 0.002 oz. in 6 in.^{3} of blood (80 mg in 100 cm^3), for example if you are running about and using up a lot of energy, stored glycogen will be released. This will be converted back into glucose to keep you going.

Diabetes

Someone who does not produce enough insulin is suffering from a disease called **diabetes**. After a meal, the level of glucose in a diabetic's blood goes on rising as there is not enough insulin to convert the glucose to glycogen. When there is 0.006 oz. of glucose in 6 in.^{3} (160 mg in 100 cm^3) of blood, it is removed from the blood by the kidneys and leaves the body in urine. Without regular meals, a diabetic's blood glucose may fall to a dangerously low level. If it falls to below 0.001 oz. glucose in 6 in.^{3} (40 mg in 100 cm^3) of blood, the person may become unconscious. This is because not enough glucose is reaching the brain cells for them to produce energy and so keep functioning properly. Some diabetics can control their illness by injecting themselves with insulin at regular intervals. They also have to be careful about the kind of foods that they eat.

* Too much growth hormone can make a person a giant and too little can make him or her a dwarf. The tallest known person was 8 feet 10 inches (2.7 meters) tall and the shortest was $27\frac{1}{2}$ inches (0.7 meters). Today, children with pituitary disorders can be treated so that they grow to normal sizes.

* The most common form of diabetes – diabetes mellitus – is also the most common defect of the endocrine system. Some mild cases can be controlled by diet alone. Special foods that contain very little sugar are available.

* Diabetes is more common in people over the age of 50 – about 15 percent of people over 50 are affected.

The Adrenal Glands

The adrenal glands are just above your kidneys. The outer part of these glands produces several hormones. One of these is called **aldosterone** and it controls the level of salts in your blood. The center part of each gland produces **adrenaline**. This is the "emergency" hormone, released when you are frightened, in danger, or under stress. It speeds up your heartbeat and your breathing rate. This means that more blood gets around the body, carrying more oxygen. It also diverts blood from your skin and intestines to your muscles and makes sure that there is plenty of glucose in the blood by converting glycogen stores to glucose. All of this means that you, and especially your muscles, have enough energy to act quickly if you have to – for example running away from something. Next time you go pale (because the blood is diverted to the muscles) and feel your heart pounding, remember that it is just your adrenaline starting to flow.

91

Repair and Recovery

Our bodies do not work perfectly all the time. Most of the things that go wrong or need repair are dealt with automatically and we know nothing about them. Sometimes, however, we feel ill as the body is fighting back strongly against a particular disorder. Most common illnesses are caused either by **bacteria** (one is a **bacterium**) or by **viruses** – tiny microorganisms which invade our bodies. Our defense or **immune** system is used to fight illnesses such as flu, food poisoning, and measles that these microorganisms cause. Certain drugs and medicines can also be used to help in the fight.

Illness in the Modern World
The most common serious illnesses in richer countries are those affecting the heart and blood circulation. Strokes, heart attacks, and high blood pressure are all usually caused by habits associated with modern life – such as stress, smoking, too much food, and too little exercise.

Cancer is another type of serious disease. It develops when certain abnormal cells divide and multiply uncontrollably. A group of these cells forms a **tumor**. The cells of a **benign** (harmless) tumor stay together in one place and the tumor can usually be removed surgically. The cells of a **malignant** tumor break away and are carried to other parts of the body by the blood or **lymph** (see page 94). The breakaway cells invade and damage healthy cells and may form new tumors.

The most common kinds of cancer start in the lungs, skin, colon, and breasts. Cancer of the white blood cells is called **leukemia**. Some cancer can be treated by removal of tumors. Other treatments are **chemotherapy** – involving the use of certain chemicals – and **radiotherapy** – where special radioactive rays are used.

Getting Older
As people grow older, some parts of their bodies may gradually wear out or work less efficiently. For example, older people can go deaf or become farsighted. Arthritis is caused by joints losing their protective covering of cartilage and some stomach ulcers are the result of damage to the digestive system. Processes of repair may take longer in older people, so that it takes them longer to recover from injuries such as broken bones. Researchers are constantly trying to discover ways in which the aging process can be slowed down.

The Invaders

Unlike diseases such as cancer and heart disease, illnesses caused by bacteria and viruses can be passed on from one person to another – they are **infectious**. Your immune system may not be able to cope with an attack of harmful bacteria or viruses if they become too powerful or there are too many of them. This is when you start to feel ill.

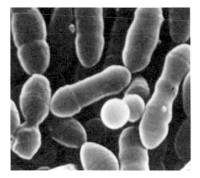

▲ **Bacteria** come in lots of different shapes. This microscope slide shows rod-shaped bacteria. A rod-shaped bacterium causes tuberculosis (TB).

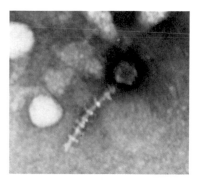

▲ **Viruses are extremely specific** – they usually only affect one host (for example humans) and often only affect particular tissues.

Bacteria

Bacteria are tiny single-celled microorganisms that can measure as little as 400 thousandths inch across. They exist all around us in the outside world and most of them are harmless. Bacteria reproduce by division. Harmful bacteria are called **pathogens**. They reproduce – often very rapidly – inside your body and may make you feel ill as they damage tissues or produce poisons. Tetanus, tonsillitis, boils, and some kinds of food poisoning are caused by bacteria.

Viruses

Viruses are much smaller than bacteria. They can only grow inside living cells which they destroy as they grow. The common cold is caused by one of many hundred different viruses which all produce the same symptoms. As body cells are invaded and damaged by viruses, the signs or symptoms of a disease develop. These symptoms may be spots, a rash, or pains. Influenza, measles, chicken pox, and polio are all diseases that are caused by viruses.

Self Defense

Bacteria and viruses can enter the body in several ways. They may be in the air that you breathe or the food and water that you eat and drink. They can enter through the skin if you cut yourself or through the openings in your body. To guard these openings, you have eyelids and tears protecting your eyes, wax in your ears, hairs in your nose, and mucus in the nose and other openings, such as the trachea. If bacteria and viruses do manage to get through these defenses, then the body has ways of fighting them. There are several kinds of white blood cells in your bloodstream. Some are called **phagocytes** and destroy bacteria by eating them. When you have an illness, extra white blood cells are manufactured. They can rush to the trouble spot and pass through capillary walls into the affected tissues.

The Lymph System

White blood cells are made in the bone marrow. Some mature in the **lymph** system. This is also called the **immune** system. Certain white blood cells called **lymphocytes** have special disease-fighting proteins on their surface. These proteins are called **antibodies** and they are made in the lymph system. When you are ill, these lymphocytes and their antibodies are released into the bloodstream. They make damaging bacteria and viruses harmless by preventing them from reproducing and by capturing them so that they can be eaten by **phagocytes**. The lymph, or immune, system can make thousands of different antibodies. Each type of bacterium or virus is tackled by a particular type of antibody.

The lymph system consists of a network of lymph vessels that reach almost every part of your body. There are lymph nodes at intervals along the vessels. The largest nodes are in your groin, armpits, and neck. These sometimes swell up when they become active in fighting an infection.

OTHER JOBS FOR THE LYMPH SYSTEM

As well as fighting disease, the lymph system has other jobs to do. Plasma leaks out of your blood capillaries while transporting substances – such as fat from your intestines – to your cells. When it is in the spaces between your cells, plasma is called **tissue fluid**.

Some of this plasma collects in the lymph vessels and rejoins the blood system through a lymph vessel near your left shoulder.

The spleen is also a part of the immune system. It stores red blood cells and also breaks down old ones.

THE IMMUNE SYSTEM

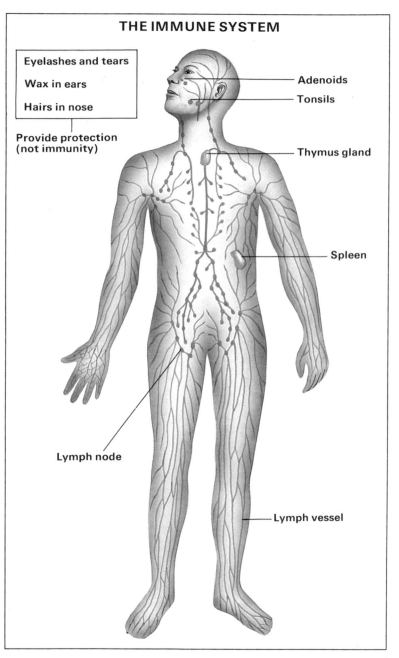

Eyelashes and tears

Wax in ears

Hairs in nose

Provide protection
(not immunity)

Adenoids

Tonsils

Thymus gland

Spleen

Lymph node

Lymph vessel

Vaccination

If your immune system has produced an antibody against a certain disease once, it will be able to produce it again very quickly if the same bacteria or virus strikes again. Because of this, you usually become protected against (immune to) a disease such as chicken pox if you have already had it once. That is how **vaccination**, also called **immunization**, works.

The substance given to you when you are vaccinated is called the **vaccine**. It contains either a harmless form of the poison which the disease-causing bacteria produce, or a dead or weakened form of the bacterium or virus. Vaccines make the body react as though it were fighting a real attack of the disease and it produces antibodies. As it has already made the antibodies, the body will be prepared for the real thing, should it strike.

Sometimes, more than one dose ("booster" doses) of a vaccine is given to people. This increases the amount of antibodies produced by the body and as a result gives extra protection.

Vaccinations are now given in most countries against serious diseases such as polio, tetanus, typhoid fever, and diptheria. You usually get most vaccinations when you are very young. They work so well that the number of reported cases of diptheria in England fell from 75,000 in 1939 to just 10 in 1970.

▼ **A young child** receiving a vaccine by injection.

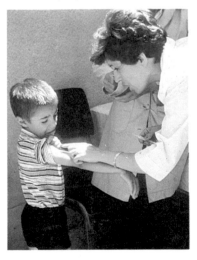

HOW DISEASES ARE SPREAD

Although we have natural defenses and vaccination to cope with illness, the best thing to do is to prevent it in the first place. There are many ways in which the harmful microorganisms that cause infectious diseases can be passed on from one person to another.

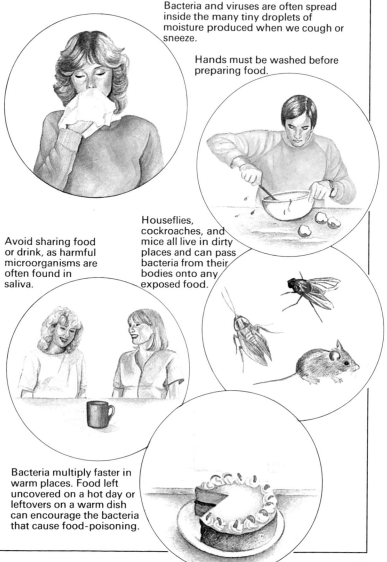

Bacteria and viruses are often spread inside the many tiny droplets of moisture produced when we cough or sneeze.

Hands must be washed before preparing food.

Houseflies, cockroaches, and mice all live in dirty places and can pass bacteria from their bodies onto any exposed food.

Avoid sharing food or drink, as harmful microorganisms are often found in saliva.

Bacteria multiply faster in warm places. Food left uncovered on a hot day or leftovers on a warm dish can encourage the bacteria that cause food-poisoning.

Symptoms and Treatment

There are four main stages to most of the infectious diseases that you can suffer from. The first stage is **getting infected**. The second is the **incubation period**, when the bacteria or viruses are multiplying inside your body. Next come the signs – **symptoms** – of the disease and finally, you should begin to **recover**.

CHICKEN POX

1. Infection. You catch chicken pox directly from someone else by breathing in tiny drops of moisture (in the air) that contain the virus.

2. Incubation. Once inside your body, the virus multiplies for about two weeks. During this time, you can still infect other people although you may not be aware that you have the disease yourself.

3. Symptoms. When these appear after the incubation period, you know for certain that you are ill. Usually, you will have a high temperature and will probably feel tired and achy. Water-filled blisters appear on your body over a period of about a week. These blisters itch, which is a sign that the body is fighting the infection.

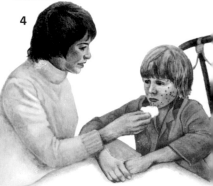

4. Treatment and Recovery. Soothing lotion is dabbed onto the spots, which gradually dry up. With rest and a good diet, you begin to feel well again.

FOOD POISONING

1. Infection. Food poisoning is caught by eating or drinking contaminated food or water. Various bacteria can cause this, for example **salmonella**. It can also be caused by various viruses and a microorganism called an entameba.

2. Incubation. Food poisoning develops very quickly. The incubation period is between 30 minutes and 2 days.

3. Symptoms. Vomiting, diarrhea, and stomachache.

4. Treatment and Recovery. Your body can usually fight off mild food poisoning quite quickly. You should make sure that you do not eat too much while you are suffering from it and avoid drinking milk. Drink plenty of water to replace what is being lost from your digestive system. If food poisoning lasts for longer than 2 days, you should see a doctor.

Body Maintenance

One of the best ways to prevent any invaders from taking a hold is to keep your body in as healthy a condition as possible. If you let yourself get out of condition, or "run down," your body is less able to fight infection. To stay healthy, the basic things you need are a good, balanced diet, sufficient sleep, fresh air, and exercise. There are also various other things that you can do to look after yourself.

● **Keeping Clean.** Wash your hands before eating and after using the toilet. Soap dissolves some of the oils on your skin where bacteria may be held.

● **Have a balanced diet** with lots of fresh fruit and vegetables.

● **Get a good night's sleep** – at least 8 hours for most adults.

● **Make sure that** you get plenty of fresh air.

● **Exercise is important.** Swimming is particularly good for you.

● **Brushing Teeth.** If you make sure that you clean your teeth regularly, bacteria and bits of food cannot build up in your mouth and cause decay.

▶ **Swimming is an enjoyable** way of exercising that is very good for promoting strong muscles, good breathing, and general staying power.

How Doctors Can Help

When you are ill, doctors can often help you by prescribing certain medicines. Many of these relieve the symptoms of the illness. For example, aspirin can help to get rid of a headache and lozenges may soothe a sore throat. **Antibiotics** are special drugs which attack bacteria without harming body cells. They either kill the bacteria or prevent them from reproducing. If you have a serious illness, doctors may decide to operate. For example, when you have appendicitis or tonsillitis, these infected and inflamed organs have to be removed by surgery.

Checkups

Providing regular checkups – medical examinations – is one way that doctors and other medical experts can help to prevent us from becoming ill by spotting any disorders at an early stage. Chest X rays can detect lung diseases such as TB before they become serious. Doctors can use machines called ultrasound scanners to follow the progress of a baby's development inside the mother (see page 106). We should make sure that we do not forget about having necessary checkups.

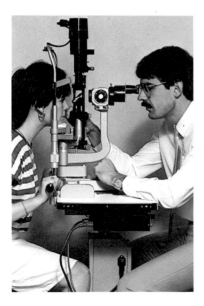

◄ **Eye tests can tell us** whether we need to wear glasses or contact lenses before our eyes become strained.

▼ **Regular visits to the dentist** allow any cavities in your teeth to be filled while they are still small.

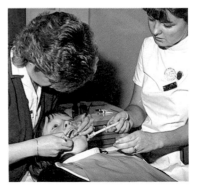

All in a Lifetime

There are many factors which influence why one person is different from another. Everyone inherits characteristics from both parents. It is the special coded instructions inside each of your cells that decide your physical appearance. They also determine some things about your personality. However, each person behaves differently because individual personality is also very strongly influenced by the way that a person has been brought up and by his or her experiences.

We change both physically and emotionally all through our lives. When we are babies and teenagers, we change at a faster rate than at any other time of our lives. When we reach puberty, our reproductive systems develop and we can have children of our own. As we grow old, our bodies begin to work more slowly and less efficiently. Eventually we will die and a new generation will be left to carry on.

A New Life

A baby begins its life when a **sperm** cell from its father meets an **egg** cell – an **ovum** (more than one are **ova**) – from its mother inside the mother's body. When the egg is **fertilized** by the sperm cell, the two cells join together to form one new cell, which starts to grow and divide. This is the beginning of the baby who will be ready to be born about 9 months later.

Egg cells come from the woman's **ovaries**. About once a month, from puberty until the age of about 45, one egg is released from one of the two ovaries. The egg then passes into one of the **Fallopian tubes**. Tiny "hairs" which line these tubes waft the egg down to the **uterus** (womb). The uterus is a hollow organ with many blood vessels and strong, muscular walls. Each month, the uterus lining thickens as it prepares to protect and nourish a fertilized ovum. If it is not fertilized, an ovum dies after about two days. The lining is now not needed, so along with the unfertilized egg and some blood, it passes out of the woman's body through the **vagina**. This loss of lining, blood, and egg is called **menstruation**, or a "period" (see page 123). Menstruation is controlled by the female hormones **progesterone** and **estrogen**. After menstruation, a new uterus lining starts to form, ready to receive the next possible fertilized egg.

Sperm are made in a man's **testes** (one is a **testis**) from puberty onward. They are stored in a tightly coiled tube called the **epididymus**. To pass to the woman's body, they travel to the **penis** through two tubes called **sperm ducts**. Sperm swim in liquids made by glands (including the **prostate**) around the **urethra** – a tube that runs from the bottom of the bladder to the tip of the penis. The mixture of sperm and liquids is called **semen**. Both semen and urine are carried by the urethra, but muscles can close the exit from the bladder to prevent the two fluids from meeting.

Sperm enter the woman's body during sexual intercourse. The man's penis becomes stiff and fits inside the woman's vagina. Semen, containing millions of sperm, is then squirted from the penis into the woman's body. The sperm are then helped toward the uterus by muscular contractions of the uterus and vagina walls, although the sperm themselves can "swim" by thrashing their tails. It takes them about 2 hours to reach the Fallopian tubes, where fertilization usually occurs. As many as 300 million sperm may start the journey, but only a few hundred reach the Fallopian tubes and only one sperm fertilizes the egg. Fertilization, or **conception**, can be prevented (see page 160).

INSIDE A WOMAN

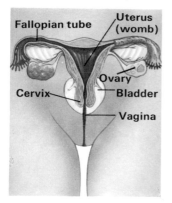

Fallopian tube
Uterus (womb)
Ovary
Cervix
Bladder
Vagina

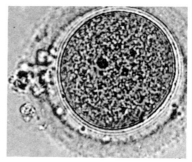

▲ An ovum is about 5 thousandths of an inch (0.1 mm) in diameter.

INSIDE A MAN

▼ Each sperm cell consists of a "head," which contains its nucleus, and a "tail." A sperm is about 2 thousands of an inch (0.05 mm) long.

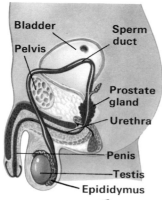

Bladder
Sperm duct
Pelvis
Prostate gland
Urethra
Penis
Testis
Epididymus

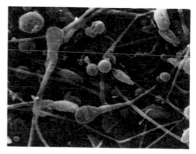

DID YOU KNOW?

✳ The uterus is only about the size and shape of a pear, but during pregnancy it can stretch to about 12 inches (30 cm) in length.

✳ The epididymus is nearly 20 feet (6 m) long if it is uncoiled.

✳ A baby girl is born with several thousand immature ova (egg cells) in her ovaries. Only a few hundred of these mature and are released during her life.

✳ The testes are held outside the body because a cooler temperature helps sperm production.

How a Baby Grows

Once a single sperm cell has penetrated an egg cell, no more sperm can enter. The nuclei of the two cells merge (fertilization) and the fertilized egg travels down the Fallopian tube toward the uterus. On the way down, it divides first into 2 cells, then into 4, then 8 and so on until a ball of at least 64 cells has been formed.

The ball of cells embeds itself in the uterus lining, which has thickened in preparation. The baby develops very quickly. After 4 weeks, its heart begins to beat. Some cells form the **umbilical cord**, which joins the baby to its mother through a special organ in the uterus called the **placenta**. Other cells form the **amnion** – a protective "bag" filled with fluid. This surrounds the baby and acts as a shock absorber to stop the baby – called an **embryo** at this stage – from being jolted.

After 8 weeks, the embryo is about 1 inch (2.5cm) long and is called a **fetus**. After about 12 weeks, it has all its organs. During the next 6 months, it grows larger and develops "details" such as fingernails and hair. At about the fifth month of development, the fetus begins to move its limbs and can be felt to kick. At this stage the baby can hear, distinguish light and dark, swallow, and suck its thumb. Some unborn babies even get hiccups. At about 6 months, the baby turns itself around in the uterus so that its head is pointing downward – the position in which it is ready to be born.

The Placenta

The placenta develops at the place where the fertilized egg first embeds itself. One side of the placenta is attached to the uterus wall. The umbilical cord links the other side of the placenta to the baby. It is through the umbilical cord that nourishment and oxygen pass to the baby from the mother's bloodstream. Also waste products and carbon dioxide from the developing baby pass back to be disposed of by the mother's body.

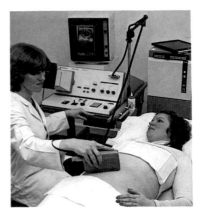

▶ **X rays can harm a developing baby** so doctors use an **ultrasound scan** machine to check its progress. This builds up a picture of the baby from high-pitched sound waves and shows it on a screen.

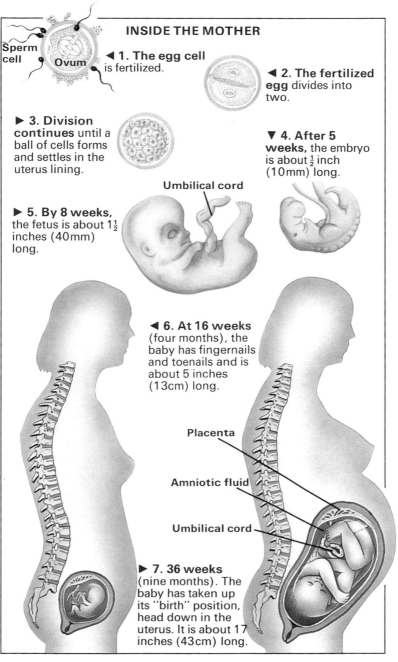

INSIDE THE MOTHER

Sperm cell **Ovum**

◀ **1. The egg cell** is fertilized.

◀ **2. The fertilized egg** divides into two.

▶ **3. Division continues** until a ball of cells forms and settles in the uterus lining.

▼ **4. After 5 weeks,** the embryo is about ½ inch (10mm) long.

Umbilical cord

▶ **5. By 8 weeks,** the fetus is about 1½ inches (40mm) long.

◀ **6. At 16 weeks** (four months), the baby has fingernails and toenails and is about 5 inches (13cm) long.

Placenta

Amniotic fluid

Umbilical cord

▶ **7. 36 weeks** (nine months). The baby has taken up its "birth" position, head down in the uterus. It is about 17 inches (43cm) long.

107

Birth

After spending about 9 months developing inside its mother, the baby is fully formed and ready to be born. The muscles of the uterus begin to contract. These contractions get stronger and each one lasts longer, in order to push the baby out of the mother's body. This is called **labor**. The opening at the bottom of the uterus – the **cervix** – widens so that the baby's head is pushed into the vagina. Then the mother uses all her strength to push downward and the baby's head emerges into the outside world. The umbilical cord is tied and cut by a doctor or midwife so that the baby begins life on its own. It is the remains of the umbilical cord that form your "belly button."

The time a baby takes to be born can be as short as 2 hours or longer than 24 hours. After the baby has been born, the placenta is also pushed out of the body through the vagina. The discarded placenta is often called the **afterbirth**. Most babies are born head first, but sometimes babies do not lie head first in the uterus just before birth and so doctors may decide to open the mother's abdomen surgically and lift the baby out. This is called a Caesarian section.

Most babies weigh about 7 pounds (3 kg) when they are born and are about 20 inches (500 mm) long. The first thing a new-born baby does is to fill its lungs with air and cry. Its lungs need to start working immediately in order to supply its body with oxygen.

▼ **Pregnant women** should continue to exercise. These women are doing special yoga exercises that help to relax them and prepare them for giving birth.

THE BIRTH OF A BABY

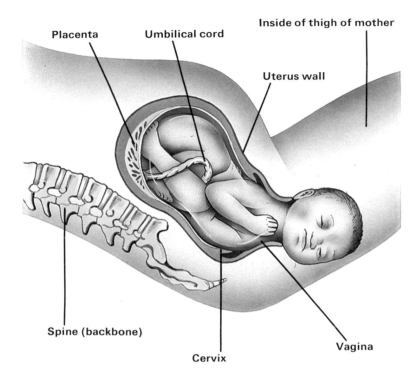

Placenta

Umbilical cord

Inside of thigh of mother

Uterus wall

Spine (backbone)

Cervix

Vagina

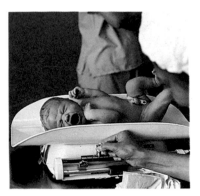

◄ **One of the first things** that happens to a baby born in a hospital is that it is carefully weighed and measured.

Looking Alike

We all inherit our physical appearance and certain other characteristics from our parents' **genes**. This is why family members tend to look like each other. We receive one set of genes from our father and another set from our mother. Each person has his or her own unique combination of genes (except for identical twins). Many characteristics are also strongly influenced by where and how we are brought up. For example, intelligence is partly inherited and partly influenced by a person's environment – his or her home and school.

Passing on Instructions

The nucleus of each human cell contains 46 (23 pairs) structures called **chromosomes**. These are made of a chemical called **DNA** (**d**eoxyribo**n**ucleic **a**cid). The units of this chemical are arranged in lots of different combinations which form coded instructions called **genes**. There are thousands of genes in each cell – the same ones in every cell – and each one determines a characteristic such as your hair color or the shape of your nose. A cell's genes contain all the instructions it needs to keep going. Sperm cells and egg cells are the only cells in the body that do not have 46 chromosomes – they have only 23. This means that when a sperm fertilizes an egg cell and they fuse, the two single sets pair up to form a full set of 46 chromosomes. Genes are able to copy themselves exactly every time a cell divides so that each cell of a developing baby has a full set of instructions – half from its mother and half from its father.

▼ **A microscope slide** of the 23 pairs of chromosomes in a human cell. Because one of these pairs has differently sized chromosomes – an "X" and a "Y" chromosome – we can tell that this cell belongs to a man.

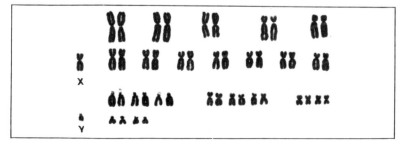

◀ **Each unit of DNA** has a structure like a twisted ladder which is called a double helix. The "rungs" of the ladder are made of various sub-units called adenine, guanine, thymine, and cytosine, arranged in pairs. The order of the rungs forms a code – a gene.

Adenine

Guanine

Thymine

Cytosine

◀ **This photograph** of the various branches of one family shows how characteristics are passed on through the generations.

111

Girl or Boy?

There is one special pair of chromosomes in each cell that decides what sex a person is. In a female, this pair consists of 2 "X" chromosomes. In a male, 1 "Y" chromosome and 1 "X" chromosome make up the pair. Sperm and egg cells have only 1 sex chromosome – half a pair – each. Egg cells always contain an "X" chromosome, whereas sperm cells can contain either an "X" or a "Y." If an egg meets an "X"-carrying sperm, then the baby produced as a result of the two cells fusing will have 2 "X" chromosomes as the pair that decide its sex. It will be a girl. If the egg cell meets a "Y"-carrying sperm, the combination produced will be "XY" – a boy.

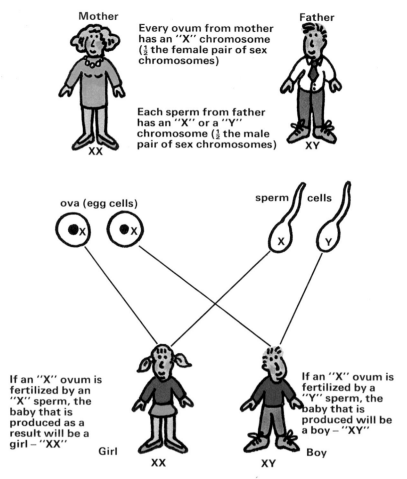

Mother

Every ovum from mother has an "X" chromosome ($\frac{1}{2}$ the female pair of sex chromosomes)

XX

Father

Each sperm from father has an "X" or a "Y" chromosome ($\frac{1}{2}$ the male pair of sex chromosomes)

XY

ova (egg cells)

sperm cells

If an "X" ovum is fertilized by an "X" sperm, the baby that is produced as a result will be a girl – "XX"

Girl

XX

If an "X" ovum is fertilized by a "Y" sperm, the baby that is produced will be a boy – "XY"

Boy

XY

Twins

There are two kinds of twins. Sometimes, the ball of cells formed when an egg is fertilized separates into two at an early stage. The two parts go on to form two babies. These are **identical** twins. They have exactly the same chromosomes and so are always the same sex as one another. They look so much alike that it may be impossible to tell them apart. The other kind of twins are called **nonidentical** or **fraternal** twins. They develop when two egg cells are released from the ovaries at the same time and are fertilized by two separate sperm cells. These twins have different chromosomes and so can be of different sexes.

◀ Identical twins.

▼ As they develop inside their mother's womb, identical twins share a placenta. Fraternal twins have one placenta each.

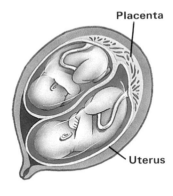

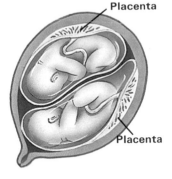

113

Which Gene?

Because half the chromosomes in your body come from the father and half from the mother, you have two genes for every characteristic. If the two genes are different, one of them may have a stronger influence than the other one. This is what happens with the genes for brown eye color and blue eye color. If someone inherits one brown eye gene from one parent and one blue eye gene from the other parent, he or she will have brown eyes because the brown eye gene has a stronger influence than the blue eye gene. The brown eye gene is called the **dominant** gene and the blue eye gene is called the **recessive** gene.

If someone inherits two blue eye genes, he or she can only have blue eyes. However, a person with blue eyes can have two brown-eyed parents because both parents may have one blue eye gene and one brown eye gene. If both parents pass on their blue eye genes, then their child will have blue eyes. You can see how this may happen below.

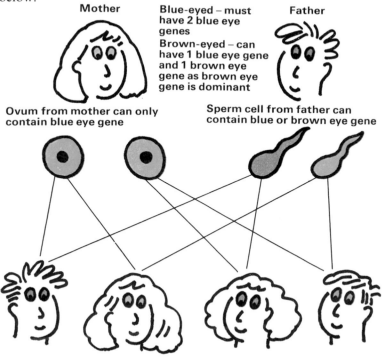

Mother

Blue-eyed – must have 2 blue eye genes
Brown-eyed – can have 1 blue eye gene and 1 brown eye gene as brown eye gene is dominant

Father

Ovum from mother can only contain blue eye gene

Sperm cell from father can contain blue or brown eye gene

Blood Groups

Sometimes one member of a pair of genes does not dominate the other and both affect a characteristic equally. Blood group is an example of this kind of characteristic. There are three different genes which decide which blood group people belong to – these genes are called **A**, **B**, and **O**. Gene "O" is dominated by the other two, but genes "A" and "B" do not dominate each other.

You can have any 2 out of these 3 genes. Which blood group you belong to depends on which 2 genes you have. There are 4 possible combinations and so 4 different blood groups.

People who have genes AA or AO belong to blood group A
People who have genes AB belong to blood group AB
People who have genes BB or BO belong to blood group B
People who have genes OO belong to blood group O

Blood group A

Blood group AB

Blood group B

Blood group O

Inheriting Problems

Occasionally, things can go wrong with genes and chromosomes. Some babies are born with a condition called **Down's Syndrome**. These children have an extra chromosome – 47 chromosomes in all. This gives them broad faces and slanting eyes and makes them mentally handicapped.

Some disorders are more commonly inherited by women than by men or the other way around. For example, **color blindness** is determined by genes on the "X" chromosome (see page 112). Because of this, color blindness is more common in men than in women. About 8 percent of men are color blind. Although it is rare for women to suffer from this, they can be **carriers** of the condition. This means that they can pass the color blindness gene on to their children although they do not suffer from it themselves.

Other inherited diseases include **hemophilia**, which also affects more men than women, and **spina bifida** ("split spine") which affects more women than men.

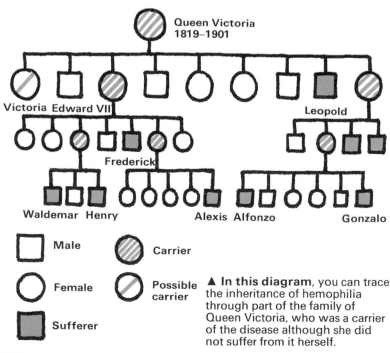

▲ **In this diagram**, you can trace the inheritance of hemophilia through part of the family of Queen Victoria, who was a carrier of the disease although she did not suffer from it herself.

MAKE YOUR OWN FAMILY TREE

You can see how certain characteristics may be inherited by picking one and seeing how it has been passed on in your own family. Do this by drawing your own family tree. Use a square to represent male members of your family and a circle for females. Some of the characteristics that you could try to trace through your family are left- and right-handedness, curly or straight hair, color of hair and eyes, and height. Some more inherited characteristics are shown below.

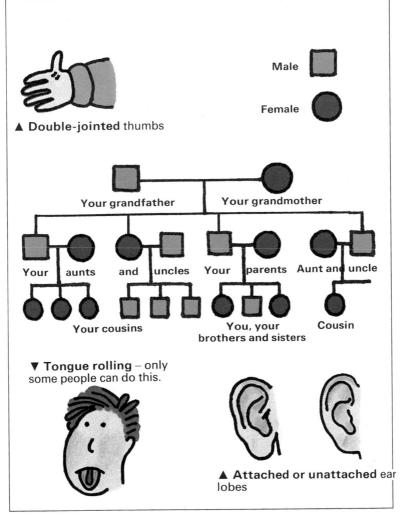

▲ **Double-jointed** thumbs

Male ☐

Female ●

Your grandfather   **Your grandmother**

Your **aunts** **and** **uncles** **Your** **parents** Aunt and uncle

Your cousins   **You, your brothers and sisters**   Cousin

▼ **Tongue rolling** – only some people can do this.

▲ **Attached or unattached** ear lobes

117

Growing Up

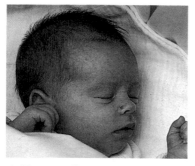

▲ **Eventually, a baby begins to sleep** all through the night and is more wakeful during the day.

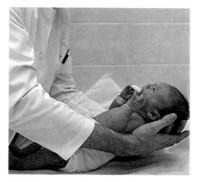

▲ **The new-born baby cannot control** the muscles that hold its head up and so the head must be supported as the baby is lifted.

A new-born baby sleeps for a lot of the time. It wakes up about every 4 hours because it needs to be fed. Hormones in the mother's body stimulate her breasts to produce milk, which contains all the nourishment that a young baby needs. Not all babies are breast-fed – some are given specially prepared milk from a bottle.

When a baby is born, its bones are made of a sort of cartilage and its skull bones are not fused together. This means that it is easier for it to squeeze down the mother's vagina. During the first two years of its life, the bones harden and the skull bones fuse.

New babies can suck, swallow, stretch, and yawn, but it is some time before they can sit up, crawl, or talk. After about two weeks, the remains of the umbilical cord fall off, leaving a scar – the navel or "belly button."

▶ **Although a new-born baby can hear well,** its eyes cannot focus properly. At first, it concentrates on looking at its parents' eyes. Soon it begins to recognize the whole face.

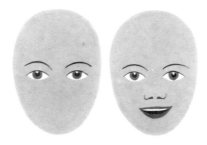

A YEAR IN THE LIFE OF ...

Each baby grows and develops at its own rate, but most babies reach certain stages at about the same time.

◄ **New-born babies have three "reflex" responses** which disappear as they grow older. The "stepping" reflex lasts for about the first 2 weeks of a baby's life. When held up-right with its feet touching a surface, a baby will auto-matically try to take steps.

▲ **The second reflex** is called the "grasp" reflex. Tiny babies will clench their fist around any object put into the palm of their hand. The grip is so strong that they can support their own weight on it. This reflex is lost after about 3 months. Babies respond with set patterns of movement when they are start-led. Often they fling their head back and their arms outward. This is the third reflex.

▲ **Most babies are given their first solid food** between the ages of 3 and 6 months.

◄ **By 6 months,** a baby has strong enough neck and back muscles to sit propped up and will be making its first sounds. "Ba," "da," "pa," and "ma" are the first words of all babies, no matter which language their parents speak. Also, around this time, a baby will have its first teeth – usually the lower front ones.

► **Between 9 and 12 months,** most babies crawl, pull themselves up, and finally walk. At one year they will have about 6 to 8 teeth and weigh 3 times more than they did at birth. Most one-year-olds can say a few words, but not until they are about 18 months old will they be able to put two simple words together to make phrases like "Daddy come" or "red car."

119

Childhood

As babies grow into children and children grow to become teenagers, many changes take place in their bodies. Not only do children grow taller, but their body proportions change. At birth, a baby's head accounts for one quarter of its body length, but in an adult the head is only an eighth of a person's height. The length of a person's arms also alters in proportion to his body size as he grows from baby to child to adult. Growth during the first two years of a person's life is very fast, but from age 3 to 10 years it is slow and steady, until adolescence, when a new spurt of rapid growth takes place.

HOW BODY PROPORTIONS CHANGE

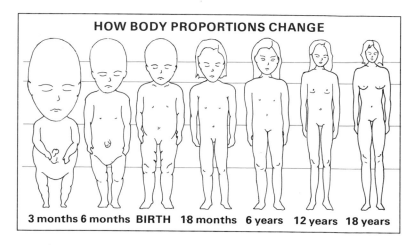

3 months 6 months BIRTH 18 months 6 years 12 years 18 years

Early Years

As a baby's muscles become more developed, he or she can perform new tasks. An 18-month-old child can climb stairs and a 2-year-old can hold a pencil to draw. By 3 years old a child is coordinated enough to copy simple shapes. People are either left-handed or right-handed. About 10 percent of boys are left-handed. The figure is lower for girls. A very small number of people can use their left and right hands equally well. They are said to be **ambidextrous**.

At around 7 or 8 years old a child's milk teeth begin to fall out as permanent teeth grow underneath. The first teeth to grow are the incisors, next come premolars at around 10–11 years old, and canines appear between the ages of 9 and 11. Molars appear between 10 and 13 years and wisdom teeth – the third set of molar type teeth – at any time between the ages of 12 and 25 years. Some people's wisdom teeth never develop.

How Old?

As a child grows older, the cartilage that made up his or her skeleton as a baby is gradually replaced by bone as the bones grow longer and thicker. It is possible to tell a child's age by looking at X rays of its bones and checking the amount of cartilage still present. An X ray of the bones of a child's hand shows the disks of cartilage still present between the joints of the child's fingers. In an adult, the disks have gone and the finger bones and hand bones have joined together, or **fused**.

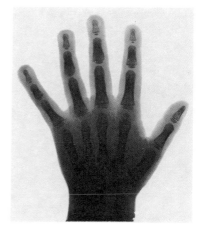

▼ **An X-ray photograph** of the hand of a 4-year-old child. There are still cartilage disks between the finger joints.

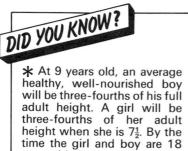

DID YOU KNOW?

✱ At 9 years old, an average healthy, well-nourished boy will be three-fourths of his full adult height. A girl will be three-fourths of her adult height when she is $7\frac{1}{2}$. By the time the girl and boy are 18 years old, the boy will be twice the height he was at 2 and the girl should be about twice the height she was at 18 months of age.

MAKE A CHART

Although children of the same age are all about the same height, there is quite a lot of variation.

Try making a chart of your friends' heights to find out the range of heights for your age group. Draw a vertical line and a horizontal line meeting at right angles to each other. Mark off the vertical line to represent the number of children of each height. Mark off the horizontal line to represent height in inches (or millimeters).

Get as many heights as you can for your age and fill in each block formed with a different color. You could do a similar chart for your friends' weight or shoe size.

Adolescence

Adolescence is the time in a person's life when he or she changes from being a child into being an adult. It all begins at puberty, when physical changes take place and the reproductive systems of boys and girls start to work, so that they are capable of producing children of their own. Adolescence continues as teenagers become more independent of their parents and start to think and act for themselves. The physical and emotional changes of adolescence are brought about by hormones.

Puberty
Puberty begins when hormones from the pituitary gland near the brain stimulate a girl's ovaries to produce the female sex hormone – estrogen – or the boy's testes to produce the male sex hormone – testosterone. No one knows exactly what makes the pituitary gland start to release its hormones. For girls, puberty usually begins between the ages of 10 and 14 years. For boys, it is normally between 12 and 15 years of age. The sex hormones change the physical appearance of boys and girls and prepare their bodies for having their own children.

▼ **Young people** usually try to widen their circle of friends by starting to go out to places like discotheques.

HOW A BOY CHANGES

● His voice becomes deeper – it "breaks."

● Hair grows in the armpits, around the genitals, and on the face and he begins to shave.

● His shoulders and chest become broader.

● The penis and testes enlarge and the testes begin to produce sperm.

● He grows taller and becomes stronger.

THE MENSTRUAL CYCLE

Each month, the ovaries release an egg cell – an ovum. The ovum travels down the Fallopian tube to the uterus. If it is not fertilized by a sperm cell, the ovum and the lining of the uterus are shed, along with a little blood. They leave the girl's body through the vagina. This menstrual bleeding is called a period and lasts for about 4 days.

Day 1
By day 28, if ovum has not been fertilized, then uterus lining is shed – period begins

Day 5
Uterus lining starts to build up to receive possible fertilized egg

Day 14
Mature ovum is released from ovary (ovulation)

Days 14–20
Most likely time for ovum to be fertilized. Lining of uterus continues to build up

The length of the whole menstrual cycle – from the beginning of one period to the start of another – varies from person to person, but the average length of time is one month. The cycle is controlled by the female hormones estrogen and progesterone.

DID YOU KNOW?

✻ Boys may continue to grow until the age of 23, whereas most girls are fully grown by about 20.

✻ Women continue to release ova from their ovaries until they are between the ages of about 42 and 52. The time in a woman's life when she stops having periods is called the **menopause**.

HOW A GIRL CHANGES

● The breasts develop.

● Hair grows around the genitals and under the arms.

● The hips broaden, so that it is easier to give birth.

● Her body shape becomes more rounded as fat is deposited around her hips and legs.

● The ovaries begin to release eggs and so periods (the menstrual cycle) begin.

Later Years

A person's body begins to age slowly after adolescence. Between the ages of 20 and 30 the body is at its strongest and the brain at its most alert. As we get older our cells renew themselves more slowly, so it takes longer to repair and replace parts of the body. Some of the signs of this are seen in older people, whose skin begins to wrinkle and muscles begin to sag. The bones of elderly people tend to shrink and the cartilage between bones may harden, making their joints stiff. One common complaint is arthritis, caused as cartilage around a joint is worn away. As we grow older our senses of sight, smell, and taste become less acute and we may grow deaf. Less blood flows to the brain, and nerve cells which die are not replaced. Some older people suffer from loss of memory. The whole body becomes less adaptable and its reactions are slower. Older people get tired more easily and do not resist disease as well as young people.

▼ **Being fit and active** should go on for as much of your life as possible.

✳ The longest a person is known to have lived is 120 years.

✳ Today in the U.S.A., the annual death rate is 9 per thousand of the population (about four persons die every minute). The birth rate is 16 per thousand (about 7 babies are born each minute).

✳ A person used to be thought dead if his or her heartbeat and breathing stopped. Today, these can be restarted using special equipment. Now doctors may use an electro-encephalograph (EEG) machine to check for any brain activity before deciding that a person had died.

MEDICAL FACTS

● Diseases, accidents, and shock all cause the heart and lungs to stop working. This is more likely to happen when you are old.

● The most common causes of death in the richer countries of the world are heart disease, strokes, and cancer.

● Since the introduction of vaccination people are less likely to die of diseases such as tuberculosis and diptheria which once caused many deaths. But diseases of the respiratory system such as pneumonia, emphysema, and bronchitis account for many deaths each year.

● No one knows why we "age."

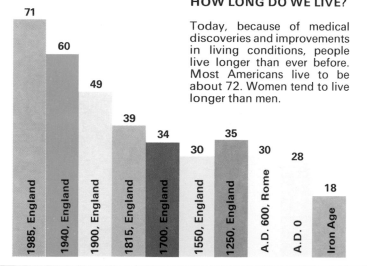

HOW LONG DO WE LIVE?

Today, because of medical discoveries and improvements in living conditions, people live longer than ever before. Most Americans live to be about 72. Women tend to live longer than men.

Year/Period	Age
1985, England	71
1940, England	60
1900, England	49
1815, England	39
1700, England	34
1550, England	30
1250, England	35
A.D. 600, Rome	30
A.D. 0	28
Iron Age	18

Making Sense of Life

Building up a relationship between ourselves and the outside world is a gradual and very complicated process. Your body, your mind, your instincts, and your experiences are working together all the time to give you your unique view of life.

Developing Skills

From the moment we are born we begin to gain skills which enable us to live and survive in the world. Early in life we begin to use our muscles and gradually start to coordinate our actions to perform more and more complicated tasks. When we are fully coordinated as children, we learn new skills in a variety of ways.

Babies begin to use their hands to pick things up when they are about 6 months old, but at this stage their fingers and hand work like a scoop. Not until the age of 9 months can they use fingers and thumbs to grip.

At one year a baby can pick things up with a finger and thumb and from this time on can hold a pencil to scribble.

By three years old a child can copy a circle but will be $4\frac{1}{2}$ years old before he or she can copy an X or a square accurately. At this age a child's brain can begin to co-ordinate what the eyes see with what it tells the muscles of the hand to do.

Older children use their experience and coordination to understand the things they see. As they grow older they may be taught to paint and draw. Then they use perspective and skill to represent what they see and how they feel about it.

Once we are fully coordinated we use various methods to learn new skills. We may learn by **doing things** – practicing and imitating what others have shown us, for example when we learn to ride a bike. We may learn by **exploring** – investigating something new and finding out how to use it, for example finding out which buttons control the TV set. We may learn by **experience** – trial and error tells us which of three similar jars contains the cookies and which contain the tea and coffee. Another important way we learn is by **being told things** or sharing the experiences of others. We do this at school or as we read a book or watch television.

▽ **Riding a bike** may seem to be a simple skill, but it requires accurate coordination of the mind and body. These cyclists, taking part in the famous Tour de France race, require skill to travel at great speeds.

Thinking Back, Looking Ahead

Things that we learn are organized by the brain and stored as **memories**. We have two types of memory: **long term** memory – which can last for many years and helps us to recognize our friends and remember where we live – and **short term** memory, which will help you play the game below.

Our memory enables us to recall what has happened to us before and to make predictions about what will happen next. It helps us to understand what is going on in the world around us. For example, if we have seen traffic lights, we know that after the green light comes amber, then red, and then cars will stop. Then we expect that we will be able to cross the road.

KIM'S GAME

▲ **Look at these objects** for a few moments. Now close your eyes or cover up the book and see how many of the objects you can remember.

Perception is a sense we develop to relate what we have seen before to what we see and expect to see again.

▶ **Perception allows us** to recognize things such as a car without seeing the whole car. As we have seen one before our brain can predict what we expect to see when only part of it is in view.

ILLUSIONS

Sometimes our predictions and expectations are not quite correct because our brain is deceived by what our eyes have seen. If you look at the pictures in this box you will see that they alter depending on what you are looking for.

Dog or pattern of black shapes?

Facing human profiles or a vase?

Communication

As we grow up, we begin to communicate. We start by crying as babies, later we make recognizable sounds and by the time we are two years old we have a vocabulary of several hundred words. By the age of four we use all the main rules of grammar.

We not only learn to communicate through the actual words we use. The way we speak adds more to what we say. We whisper a secret, shout when we are angry, and talk loudly if we want to be sure we are heard. Emphasis and tone of voice also alter the meaning of words.

▲ **Blind people** "read" books in the form of braille. This is patterns of tiny raised bumps which represent letters and words.

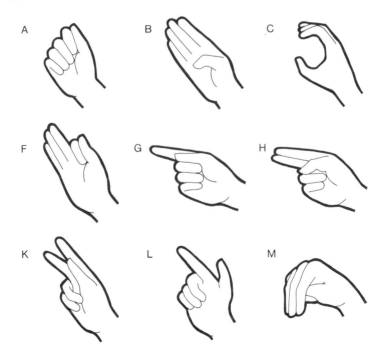

Speaking Without Words

We do not have to use words at all. Deaf people who cannot speak communicate by using signs or by reading lips. We communicate through reading books and blind people use braille. People who do not speak the same language can communicate using signs and gestures.

Gestures of our hands, eyebrows, and head say a lot about how we feel. The way we stand or sit can indicate whether we feel tired or bored and whether or not we feel confident or cautious. A confident person tends to stand up straight but a nervous one may slouch.

◄ **People who cannot speak** use a language called "signing." This involves using the hands and fingers to represent letters and words.

▶ **Look at this sequence** of photographs and see if you can work out what is happening from the people's gestures and facial expressions.

People have always needed to communicate and express themselves. Over the centuries, many different ways have been found to do this – from cave paintings to computers. On these pages are some of the ways that people have developed. See how many more you can think of.

▼ **Semaphore** is a way of communicating over a distance, by using special flags.

◄ **This ancient clay tablet** is from the Middle East and is about 5,000 years old. The writing on it is in the form of simple pictures.

✱ There are around 600,000 words in the English language. An average person uses only a few thousand of these and a person can be fluent in English knowing only 2,000 words. Professional writers know more words than average but even they only use 50,000 – less than 10 percent of the words available.

✱ The commonest language is Mandarin, spoken by an estimated 600 million people. English is the next most common. It is spoken by about 360 million people.

✱ There are 5,000 different languages in the world.

大明嘉
靖年製

▲ **Chinese writing** looks rather like pictures. This is the signature of a sixteenth-century Chinese artist.

▼ **Painters often try to communicate** certain ideas through their work. This painting of a tree, by the Dutch artist Piet Mondrian, uses slightly "unrealistic" colors and is a little abstract. However, because our brains can cope with complicated ideas, we can accept this quite easily.

Human Machines

People live in environments as different as the frozen wastes of the Arctic and the steaming jungles of South America. The human body can adjust to cope with most of the climatic conditions on earth, keeping the body temperature constant at 98.6°F (37° C), and all of the body's systems working.

New inventions and the discoveries of modern science have given people the ability to extend the range of places in which they can survive and the number of things that the human body can achieve. People cannot live in space because the atmosphere does not contain oxygen and because the environment is too harsh. Space suits protect astronauts' bodies and, enclosed in them, they can receive a supply of oxygen so that they can breathe while on "space walks." Specially weighted suits even allow astronauts to walk on the moon where the natural gravity does not hold them down. Exploration of the deep seas has been made possible by the development of sophisticated underwater vehicles and diving suits which protect the human body from the great pressure many feet down.

▼ **Because of special suits** like this one, scientists can survive in environments beyond our planet and carry out valuable research.

HOT AND COLD

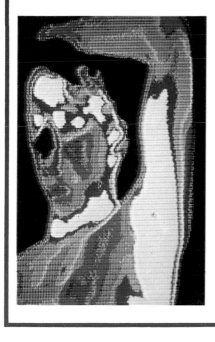

◄ **Sophisticated machines called thermographs** produce special pictures by using infrared film. This picture shows the variation in heat emitted by different areas of the body. With most thermographs, the hottest areas show up as being red on the picture, and the coldest appear blue.

The human brain is able to remember, reason, plan, and forget. Modern computers have memories programmed by just a few people. Although computers cannot think as we do, one computer can store more information in its memory than hundreds of people put together.

Human eyes and ears are vital senses, but many things that we use every day extend our natural abilities. The telephone and radio allow us to hear the voices of people speaking many thousands of miles away. Satellites transmit television pictures of things on the other side of the world for us to see. Cameras using infrared film, which is sensitive to heat rays, enable us to "see" very small differences in temperature, and special instruments called Geiger counters can turn invisible radioactive waves into sounds.

Who knows what the human body will be able to do next?

Body Facts

Who invented the stethoscope? What does acupuncture involve? Why do some people blush? In this reference section you can use the **Medicine and History** pages and the comprehensive **Glossary** to find out. Then there is an **Index** for the whole book.

The seventeenth-century Dutch anatomist Nicholaes Tulp at work in Rembrandt's painting – "The Anatomy Lesson."

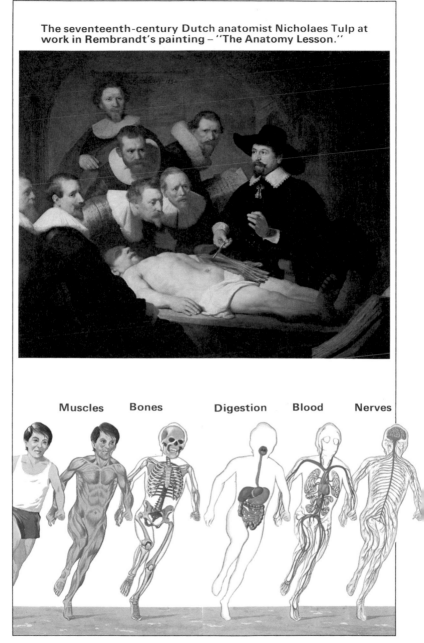

Muscles   Bones   Digestion   Blood   Nerves

Medicine and History

3000 B.C. The first civilization with prescriptions for medicines was Mesopotamia (modern day Iraq). Instructions on how to use drugs such as opium and belladonna were written on wax tablets.

400 B.C. The Ancient Greeks were very interested in the body and how it worked. One of their most famous doctors at this time was Hippocrates. He knew the importance of fresh air, good food, and rest in healing the body. He laid down certain rules

▲ **Vesalius's study** of the human body through dissection enabled him to make many precise and useful drawings.

called the Hippocratic Oath for doctors to obey. Doctors still follow rules based on it today.

A.D. 14 Around this time the Romans are known to have had a hospital near the site of a battle. Ancient Rome had a system of sewers and by the fourth century A.D. Rome is thought to have had 144 flushing lavatories.

1543 Andreas Vesalius, a Flemish doctor, made the first accurate studies of the human body. He published a book on anatomy called *The Working of the Human Body*. Examining the body was frowned on at this time and so Vesalius used stolen corpses for his research.

1600 The microscope was invented by Hans and Zacharias Janseen around this time. It became well known in 1665 through the work of Robert Hooke in England and soon afterward Van Leeuwenhoek saw the first microorganisms in a sample of his own saliva.

In the early 1600s Sanctorius invented the first thermometer for taking human temperatures, and quinine was discovered as a treatment for malaria in South America.

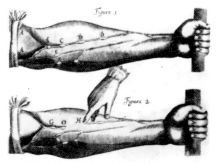

◀ **William Harvey** was the first to suggest that the heart works like a pump. This illustration appeared in his book on blood circulation.

1628 William Harvey, a physician to James I, wrote a book called *Concerning the Motion of the Heart and Blood.* It was the first time that the circulation of the blood had been described.

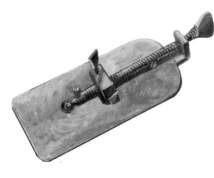

▲ **Van Leeuwenhoek's microscope** was very simple, but powerful enough to see bacteria.

▶ **The thermometer** invented by Sanctorius was an adaptation of Galileo's thermoscope (1592).

Medicine and History

1796 Edward Jenner discovered that people who caught a mild disease called cowpox never caught smallpox. He took pus from a cowpox sore on the hand of a dairymaid and injected it into the arm of a boy. When Jenner injected smallpox virus later, the boy did not become ill. Edward Jenner had discovered vaccination.

1816 René Laennec made one of the first stethoscopes from rolled paper. Later, a wooden one was made in England by John Elliotson. At first, stethoscopes had only one earpiece, but in the year 1850 the biaural stethoscope with two earpieces was developed.

1844 Horace Wells, an American dentist, used nitrous oxide, or "laughing gas," to put his patients to sleep while he gave them treatment. Later (in 1846) another American dentist, William Morton, used the gas ether as an anesthetic during an operation. Before this time patients were either made drunk before operations or were held down by doctors' assistants.

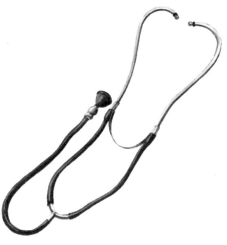

▲ **Laennec's paper stethoscope.** More familiar is the biaural stethoscope (right) used by doctors today for examining the heart and lungs.

142

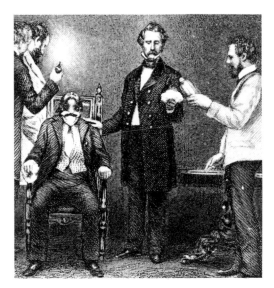

◄ **William Morton,** the American dentist, gives ether to a patient as an anesthetic.

▼ **An anesthetist's equipment** in the 1800s included an inhaler for the patient's face and a simple drop bottle.

1847 Dr. James Simpson first used chloroform as an anesthetic. Later (in 1853) Queen Victoria's doctor, John Snow, used chloroform during the birth of the queen's seventh child. He later developed an inhaler so that the chloroform could be given in measured amounts.

143

▶ **Lister developed a carbolic spray** (1875) to kill harmful microorganisms in the air. It worked by means of a steam kettle.

1860 Joseph Lister began using weak carbolic acid as an antiseptic after he realized that many people were dying after operations because they caught infections. He knew from reading the work of Louis Pasteur that there were harmful microorganisms in the air, in water, and on clothing, so he used carbolic acid to clean his surgical instruments, bandages, clothes, and hands. Lister was also the first doctor to use catgut (strips from the intestines of cats) to stitch up wounds.

1864 The Red Cross Society was founded in Geneva. In wartime, the Red Cross takes care of injured soldiers and prisoners and it also helps in the care and rescue of people affected by floods, earthquakes, and other natural disasters.

1865 In the early 1860s, Louis Pasteur discovered that bacteria in the air cause perishable food to go bad. He therefore invented "pasteurization." This process involved treating food with heat to kill the bacteria and so prevent the food from decaying quickly.

Between 1879 and 1885 he found ways of weakening harmful microorganisms so that they could be made into vaccines. He used vaccines against cholera, rabies, anthrax, and swine plague.

▲ **Louis Pasteur** successfully treated a child bitten by a rabid dog with his vaccination against rabies in 1885. Pasteur's different types of vaccines saved many lives.

1870 Elizabeth Garrett Anderson became the first woman doctor.

1883 Robert Koch, a German scientist, developed techniques for the study of bacteria. He also established certain rules for identifying the bacteria that cause particular diseases. He is most famous for the discovery of the bacterium that causes tuberculosis (TB).

145

◀ **Anesthetics and even aspirin** were not developed until the nineteenth century. This illustration of an eighteenth-century French dentist at work demonstrates how painful a visit to the dentist could be.

1883 Cocaine was used as a local anesthetic for the first time, during an eye operation. Later it was used by dentists who wished to treat just a small area of a person's mouth. Today, dentists use procaine, nupercaine, and amethocaine. These anesthetics act like cocaine but are not habit forming.

1886 The increasing knowledge of microorganisms and disease led to the introduction of sterilization of medical instruments using steam. Also, from this time surgeons wore masks, gowns, and capes when they carried out operations.

1895 Wilhelm Röntgen discovered X rays as a way of looking at bones. Later it was discovered that if a person is fed a meal of barium sulphate, it is possible to see the body's organs as the barium casts a shadow on the X-ray plate.

1895 Sigmund Freud, an Austrian psychiatrist, founded psychoanalysis. He treated mental disorders by encouraging his patients to look back to their childhood in an attempt to understand their behavior and feelings. He believed that dreams were a clue to the unconscious and published *The Interpretation of Dreams* in 1900.

▼ **William Röntgen**
demonstrates his invention – the X ray.

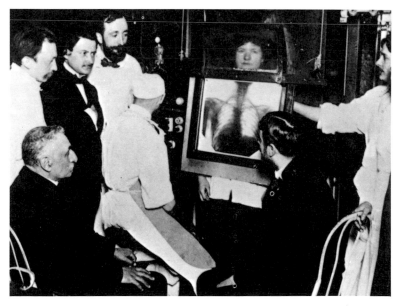

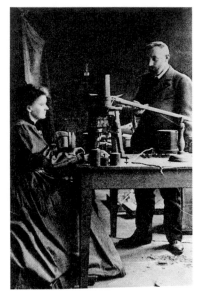

▲ Pierre and Marie Curie
produced radium from a mineral
called pitchblende.

used to treat cancer. Today,
cobalt 60 is used for such treatment instead of radium.

1910 The four blood groups
A, AB, B, and O were discovered
by Dr. Karl Landsteiner. The
first blood transfusion was given
by Dr. James Blundell in 1818,
but until blood groups were discovered there were many failures
using transfusions.

1920 The first EEG (electroencephalograph) machine was
developed to detect and record
electrical activity in the brain.

1928 Sir Alexander Fleming
discovered penicillin, a mold
which could kill bacteria. This
was the first antibiotic. However,
Fleming could not find a way of
making penicillin in large
amounts. It was not until 1938
that Howard Floery and Ernst
Chain found a way to make pure
penicillin in large quantities.

1928 The Drinker respirator
(Iron Lung) was developed in
Boston, Massachusetts. It was
first used successfully in 1932 to
save the life of a boy with
paralysis.

1898 Sir Ronald Ross – a
British physician born in India –
discovered that malaria is spread
by mosquitoes.

1902 Marie and Pierre Curie
discovered radium and polonium
– two radioactive substances
which produce rays that can be

1943 The first mass X-ray unit
was set up in England.

1944 The first kidney machine was developed by Dr. Wilhelm Kolff, in secret, during the German occupation of Holland. This was the first machine to actually take the place of a major organ of the body.

1950 The first kidney transplant was performed by Dr. R. Lawler in Chicago.

1952 Jonas Salk, an American microbiologist, produced the first vaccine that prevented polio. Robert Koch and John Enders had earlier contributed to the effort by cultivating bacteria and growing polio viruses.

Mass vaccination against polio began in the mid 1950s. By 1960 the occurrence of polio had been greatly reduced.

▲ **The process performed** by a kidney machine, when a person's kidneys fail, is called renal dialysis.

1954 The heart-lung machine was developed to take the place of a person's heart during heart surgery.

149

Medicine and History

▼ The head of an endoscope may be only ¼ inch (6mm) wide.

1969 The Hanson family quintuplets were born in Rayleigh, Essex, Great Britain. These were the first quintuplets to survive into childhood.

1973 The CAT scanner was invented by Godfrey Hounsfield (of EMI) for taking very detailed X rays of fine "slices" of the body (see page 11).

▼ Dr. Christiaan Barnard – the first person to carry out a successful human heart transplant – with one of his patients.

1958 The first internal heart pacemaker was fitted to Arne Larsson in Stockholm by Dr. A. Stenning.

1958 The endoscope (see page 10) was developed. This meant that doctors could examine the internal parts of the body without having to cut the patient open.

1967 The first human heart transplant was performed by Dr. Christiaan Barnard in South Africa. The heart was given to Louis Washkansky, who survived for 18 days. Hundreds of heart transplants have been successfully performed since.

1976 Dr. G. Shannon fitted a bionic, transistorized artificial arm to a car accident victim in Queensland, Australia.

1978 Louise Brown, the world's first "test-tube" baby, was born in Oldham, Lancashire, Great Britain. Her mother's ovum was taken out and fertilized in a laboratory run by Robert Edwards and Patrick Steptoe. The fertilized ovum was then placed in the mother's uterus to develop normally.

1981 Professor Norman Shumway performed the first heart and lung transplant in California.

1982 The first artificial heart transplant was carried out in the U.S.A. The patient's name was Barney Clarke.

▼ **Robert Edwards and Patrick Steptoe** – pioneers of the research that produced the world's first "test-tube" baby.

Glossary

In this alphabetical glossary, words and terms in *italics* also have their own separate entry.

A

Abcess A painful, red, swollen area inside the body, filled with pus and caused by *bacteria*. A "gumboil" is a type of abcess caused by an infected tooth.

Acne Spots, blackheads, or whiteheads caused by inflammation of the oil glands in the skin. Four out of five teenagers suffer from acne. Usually it affects the face, shoulders, chest, and back. It can be partly prevented by eating less fatty foods, sugar, and possibly chocolate.

Acupuncture A form of medical treatment which originated in China 5,000 years ago. It aims to relieve pain and illness by the insertion of 2–3 inch (5–8 cm) needles along the body "meridians" where the Chinese believe the life forces flow. Acupuncture can be used as an alternative form of *anesthetic* or to treat illnesses such as migraine, indigestion, or rheumatism.

Adam's apple The name given to the piece of *cartilage* which sticks out over the front of the *larynx*. It can sometimes be seen at the front of the neck. A man's Adam's apple is larger than a woman's because his vocal cords and larynx are larger.

Adenoids Small *glands* made of *lymph* tissue at the back of the nasal passages. Together with the *tonsils* they help to protect the lungs from infection. Adenoids become swollen when you have a nose or throat infection and can block your nose so that you have to breathe through your mouth.

Adrenaline A *hormone* released by the adrenal glands as a result of fear, anger, or shock. It makes the heart beat faster, increases *blood pressure,* and enables *muscles* to work harder and longer.

Allergy A reaction such as a running nose, rash, or wheezing caused when people are sensitive to certain substances. Some people are allergic to particular foods such as milk, eggs, wheat, and strawberries. Hay fever is caused by pollen. People who suffer from this develop red watering eyes and sneeze a lot. At least one person in ten suffers from an allergy occasionally.

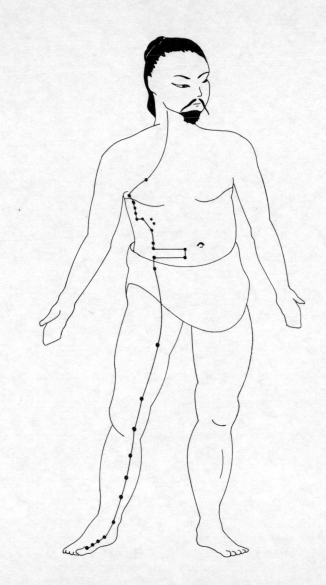

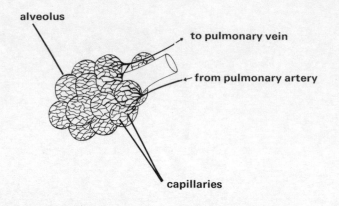

alveolus

to pulmonary vein

from pulmonary artery

capillaries

Alveoli Tiny air sacs in the lungs where oxygen is collected by the blood.

Amino acids The chemical subunits which make up *proteins*. When foods containing protein are digested (broken down), the proteins are separated into amino acids which are transported around the body. The amino acids are assembled into new proteins in the cells. Although there are millions of different proteins, there are only 20 basic amino acids.

Anemia A disorder of the blood caused by having too little *hemoglobin*. This means that the blood's oxygen-carrying capacity is reduced. An anemic person may look pale and feel tired or dizzy.

Anesthetic A substance which removes a person's sensitivity to pain. A general anesthetic produces a lack of feeling and puts a person to sleep before an operation. A local anesthetic numbs a small area. For example, dentists inject local anesthetics to deaden nerves for one or two hours, so that they can work on just one tooth.

Anorexia nervosa An illness usually affecting young women. People with anorexia nervosa think that they are overweight even though they are not, lose their appetite, and eat very little. A steady loss of weight results and *menstruation* may stop.

Antibiotics Drugs which can kill *bacteria* by preventing them from growing or reproducing.

Common antibiotics are penicillin, streptomycin, and tetracyclin. Each kind works best against certain bacteria. For example, streptomycin kills tuberculosis bacteria. Antibiotics do not kill *viruses* and so cannot cure virus diseases such as colds.

Antibodies Substances produced by the body's immune system. They destroy harmful *bacteria* and *viruses* and neutralize the poisons which they produce. Some antibodies never disappear from the body once they have been produced. This is why you develop immunity to some diseases (for example, measles and mumps) after you have had them once.

Antiseptics Substances which kill certain *microorganisms* or slow down their growth. They can be used to clean wounds and sterilize doctors' instruments, and as household disinfectants.

Aorta The main *artery* which leaves the left *ventricle* of the heart.

Appendix The short section of the digestive system where the small and large *intestines* join. It is about 4 inches (10 cm) long and forms a dead-ending branch off the intestine. It is not used in human digestion. "Appendicitis" occurs when the appendix becomes inflamed or infected and has to be removed.

Artery Any blood vessel which carries blood away from the heart to the rest of the body. The largest artery is the *aorta* which is 1 inch (2.5 cm) across.

Asthma Difficulty in breathing, usually caused by an *allergy* or infection. People who have attacks of asthma begin to wheeze or cough and feel a tightening of their chests. Asthma can be made worse by stress or by certain weather conditions. It is usually treated by inhaling medicated sprays.

Athlete's foot An infection of the skin between the toes caused by a fungus. The skin becomes scaly or blistered and the condition is made worse by perspiration or damp. People who suffer from athlete's foot should clean and dry their skin and apply special powders or cream.

Atrium One of the two upper chambers of the heart which receives blood from the *veins* and pumps it to the *ventricles*.

Auricle Another word for *atrium*.

Autonomic nervous system The part of your nervous system which controls "automatic" actions such as breathing and heartbeat.

Axon The long fiber of a *nerve* cell which carries messages away from the nerve cell body.

B

Backbone Another word for the spine or vertebral column.

Bacteria Microscopic one-celled living organisms found all around us – in water, soil, and on our bodies. Most bacteria are harmless. However a few pathogenic (disease-causing) bacteria result in diseases such as tuberculosis (TB), tetanus, pneumonia, and boils.

BCG A vaccination used to *immunize* people against tuber-

The vertebrae of the backbone enclose and so protect the spinal cord as beads fit around a string.

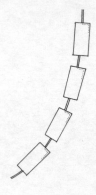

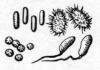

Bacteria come in lots of different shapes and sizes.

culosis. It is named after the man who discovered it, the French bacteriologist, Bacille Calmette-Guerin. BCG vaccination is given to people who are likely to come into contact with tuberculosis and to people who are not resistant to the disease. Children are tested at the age of about 12 years to see if they are resistant.

Benign A word used to describe a growth or *tumor* which is harmless and not likely to get worse. If a benign tumor is removed it is not likely to grow again. The opposite of benign is *malignant*.

156

Biceps The *muscle* in the upper arm which contracts when you bend your arm. It is attached to the shoulder by two *tendons* and to the lower arm by just one *tendon*. The large muscle behind the *femur* (thigh bone) is also attached like this and is also called the biceps.

Bile A green liquid produced by the *liver* which helps to digest fat in the small *intestine*. Bile is stored in the *gall bladder*.

Bladder A muscular bag which collects urine produced by the *kidneys*. An adult's bladder can hold about $\frac{3}{4}$ pint (400cc) of urine. Urine is released when the *sphincter* muscle around the tube (the *urethra*) which leads out of the bladder relaxes. You release urine when the bladder fills up and you feel uncomfortable.

Blind spot The place on the *retina* from which the optic nerve leads to the brain. The blind spot has no *rods* or *cones*.

Blood pressure Blood pressure in the blood vessels depends on how strongly the heart pumps and how much the blood vessels resist the blood flowing through them. Blood pressure is measured using a sphygmomanometer. First, the pressure is measured as the heart contracts. This is called the systolic pressure. Then the diastolic pressure is measured as it relaxes. The results are shown as two figures given in millimeters of mercury – a young person's blood pressure is about 120/80. Blood pressure rises as you get older.

Blushing A reddening of the skin, especially the cheeks. It is caused by blood flowing to the skin *capillaries* when you are angry or embarrassed.

Bowel Usually used as another name for the large *intestine* where *feces* (undigested food) are stored before being passed out of the body.

Bronchus One of the branches of the windpipe or *trachea* leading to, and dividing inside, the lungs. The right bronchus – one of the two main branches off the windpipe – is about 1 inch (2.5cm) long before it enters the right lung and begins to divide into many more bronchi and eventually into bronchioles. The left bronchus is twice this length. If the bronchi become infected and inflamed the disease is called bronchitis.

Bruise A blue-black mark on the skin which is caused by a bang or pressure. Blood vessels under the skin are damaged and some blood leaks out before the bruise is healed. A "black eye" is a particularly bad kind of bruise because the skin around the eye is thin and loose and there are lots of *capillaries* there.

C

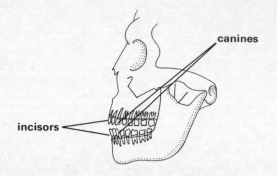

canines

incisors

Caesarian section Sometimes, if a pregnant woman is ill or has a large baby, doctors may decide to deliver the baby by Caesarian section. The doctor makes a cut in the mother's abdomen and *uterus* and lifts the baby out.

Cancer A disease which can affect almost any part of the body. Cancer begins when some abnormal or *malignant* cells begin to grow and form a *tumor* or swelling which damages other cells. Some cells of the tumor may break off and begin another tumor.

Cancer can sometimes be successfully treated by operations to remove the tumor. It may also be treated by chemotherapy (chemical means) or radiotherapy (by X rays or radiation). Cancer is not infectious.

Canines The pointed teeth that are on each side of your *incisors*. They are sometimes called "eye" teeth.

Capillary A tiny blood vessel. Capillaries connect the small branches of *arteries* with small branches of *veins* and carry blood to all the cells of the body.

Carbohydrates With *protein* and *fats* these form one of the three main groups of foods. They supply the energy we need to stay alive. Carbohydrates are digested (broken down) in the body to *glucose* which can be carried by the blood. All carbohydrates come from plants. Sugars, such as fructose, glucose, and sucrose (table sugar) are all carbohydrates and so is starch. Foods which contain a lot of carbohydrate are bread, cereals, potatoes, and rice. Too many carbohydrates can make you fat, so people trying to lose weight often reduce the amounts of these foods in their diet.

Cardiac Referring to the heart. For example – cardiac *muscle*.

Cartilage The soft, elastic white *tissue* which covers the ends of bones at the *joints*. It is also found in the nose, ear lobes, and *larynx*. The disks between the vertebrae are made of cartilage and so is the skeleton of an unborn baby.

Cell A cell is the basic living unit which makes up the body. There are many different shapes and sizes of cells; for example – bone cells, skin cells, and nerve cells. Although these various types of cells look very different they all have the same basic contents. Groups of the same cells make up *tissues*.

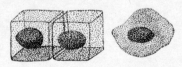

2 different shapes of epithelial cells

Central nervous system The brain and the *spinal cord*.

Cerebellum The area of the brain which controls and coordinates body movements.

Cholesterol A fatty substance made by the *liver* and adrenal *glands*. It is found throughout the body and makes up 14 percent (dry weight) of the brain and *spinal cord*. Hardening of the *arteries* in older people is caused when fat deposits, including cholesterol, in the arteries attract calcium. This makes the arteries less flexible.

Chromosome One of the 46 structures in the nucleus of every cell. Chromosomes are made of a special chemical called *DNA*. They carry the *genes* which determine all our inherited characteristics such as eye color, hair type, and sex.

Cochlea The coiled part of the inner ear which looks like a snail shell and contains the receptors for hearing.

Colon Usually used to mean the lower part of the large *intestine*. In the colon, water is absorbed from undigested food, leaving *feces*.

Cone One of the light-sensitive receptor cells found in the *retina* of the eye. Cones give you color vision.

Contraception The prevention of *fertilization* or pregnancy. There are several ways of doing this:

1. The rhythm method is a "natural" method in which couples do not have intercourse for about 10 days of the menstrual cycle because during this time the *ovum* may be fertilized.

2. "The pill" contains female sex hormones and works by "fooling" the woman's body into thinking that she is pregnant so that she does not release any ova.

3. Some contraceptives prevent *sperm* reaching the ovum by forming a barrier between them. The diaphragm or cap is a rubber device worn by a woman and a rubber sheath or condom is worn by a man.

4. IUDs (**I**ntra-**u**terine **d**evices) are coils or loops of metal or plastic which are inserted into the *uterus* to prevent a fertilized ovum from embedding in the uterus lining.

Cornea The transparent front layer of the eyeball. It allows light to enter the eye and helps to focus light rays on the *retina*.

Coronary Referring to the blood vessels that supply the heart. Coronary *arteries* over the surface of the heart provide oxygen for its cells. The word is also used sometimes to mean a heart attack.

Corpuscle Another name for a *red* or *white blood cell*.

Cortex The outer layer of the brain or "gray matter." Made up of millions of nerve cells, it is reponsible for all thinking processes. The word is also used to describe parts of other organs such as part of the *kidneys*.

Cramp Pain in a *muscle* caused when it contracts and goes into a spasm, staying contracted for a long time. You may get a cramp in your leg muscles after a lot of exercise. Massage can help relieve a cramp.

Cuticle Another name for the outer layer of the skin or epidermis. It is also the thin layer of epidermis cells which are attached to the base of the nails.

cortex

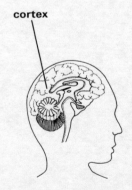

D

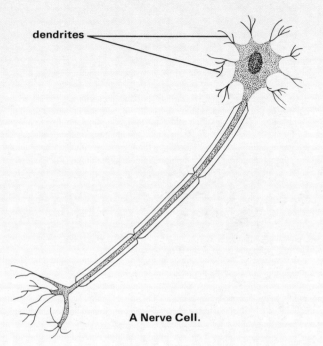

dendrites

A Nerve Cell.

Dandruff Small flakes of dead skin in the hair, caused by a disorder of the glands in the scalp which secrete sebum (oil). There may be too little sebum – giving dry brittle hair – or too much oil – giving greasy hair and yellow flakes of dandruff.

Dendrite One of the short fibers of a nerve cell which carries messages toward the cell body.

Dentine The hard bone-like material which makes up a tooth. It is covered by a protective layer of *enamel* in the part of the tooth (called the crown) which we can see above the gum.

Dermis The lower living layer of the skin – just below the epidermis – which contains nerves, blood vessels, hair follicles, and sweat glands.

Diabetes An illness in which a person does not produce enough *insulin* and so cannot control the level of sugar *(glucose)* in their blood. After a meal the level of glucose in a diabetic's blood rises, and without insulin it is not removed to be stored as glycogen. Glucose accumulates and eventually is passed out, unused, in urine. Diabetes can be treated by injecting extra insulin into the body.

Diaphragm The flat *muscle* which separates the chest from the abdomen. The diaphragm flattens as you breathe in and your chest cavity expands. As you breathe out it arches up to force air out of your lungs.

Diptheria A serious disease of the throat caused by *bacteria*. A gray *membrane* forms in the throat and the bacteria produce powerful poisons which affect the whole body.

Diptheria used to be a very common cause of death among children, but today it is rare and most children are vaccinated against it.

DNA **D**eoxyribo**n**ucleic **a**cid is the very complicated chemical which makes up our *chromosomes* and carries – as *genes* – all the information which we inherit from our parents. DNA is found in the nucleus of every cell in our bodies and it controls the way each cell works.

Down's Syndrome An inherited condition caused by having an extra *chromosome*, 47 instead of the normal 46. A Down's Syndrome child has a short, broad face, slanted eyes, short fingers, and is mentally retarded. Mothers over 40 years of age are more likely to have a baby with this condition.

Duodenum This 12 inch (30 cm) section of the small *intestine* leads out of the stomach and is where the digestion of food starts.

Dyslexia The inability to read properly due to a disorder of the brain. Dyslexics confuse letters and words but are not necessarily of low intelligence.

E

Eardrum (Tympanum). The thin membrane at the end of the ear canal. It vibrates and passes sound on to the inner ear where receptor cells respond and send messages to the brain.

ECG (Electrocardiogram). A graph made by amplifying the electrical impulses produced by the heart. Examining the pattern of the impulses enables a doctor to see how healthy a person's heart is. For example, if one chamber of the heart becomes enlarged it may change the shape of the electrocardiogram.

Eczema Inflammation of the skin (itchy rash and blisters) which can be caused by an allergic reaction to substances or irritation by them, or by skin that is very oily or very dry.

Enamel The hard protective covering of the teeth (see *dentine*).

Endocrine gland Glands which produce *hormones*.

Enzymes Chemical substances found in the body which speed up its life processes. Thousands of different enzymes control many different processes.

Particular digestive enzymes help to break down certain types of food, for example, ptyalin (found in saliva) helps to digest *carbohydrates*. Pepsin, which is an enzyme found in the stomach, helps to digest *protein*.

Epidermis See *cuticle*.

Epiglottis A small flap of *cartilage* that slants upward at the back of the tongue. During swallowing, it is pushed against the opening to the *trachea* and prevents food going "down the wrong way."

Erythrocyte Another word for a *red blood cell*.

Esophagus The 10 inch (25 cm) long tube which carries food from the mouth to the stomach. It takes about 5 seconds for food to travel down the esophagus.

Estrogen The female sex *hormone* made in a woman's *ovaries*. Estrogen causes breasts and other female characteristics to develop at *puberty* and it also stimulates the thickening of the lining of the *uterus* during the menstrual cycle.

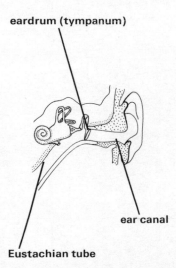

eardrum (tympanum)

ear canal

Eustachian tube

163

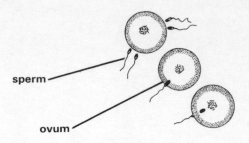

Feritilization

are about 4 inches (10cm) long and it is usually inside them that an ovum is fertilized.

Fats One of the important types of food we need in our diets, fats supply the body with energy and carry fat-soluble *vitamins* A and D. Fats may be solids like butter, or liquids like cooking oil. The digestion of fat begins in the *duodenum* and is completed in the remainder of the small intestine. Digested fats are carried in the *lymph* system. Too much fat in your diet can make you overweight because fat can be stored in your body in adipose tissue.

Eustachian tube The tube which connects the middle ear with the throat. It helps to keep the pressure inside the ear the same on both sides of the eardrum. The tube opens when you swallow. This can cause your ears to "pop" if the air pressure around you is changing.

Changes in air pressure occur, for example, when you take off in an airplane or climb a mountain.

F

Fallopian tubes (or oviducts). The tubes which lead from the *ovaries* to the *uterus*. The tubes

Feces The waste material which leaves the body after food has been digested. Feces contain undigested food and also worn-out cells from the *intestine*, mucus, secretions containing waste from your *liver,* and *bacteria*. The material in feces varies from day to day, depending on what type of food you have eaten.

Femur Thigh bone – the longest, strongest bone in the body.

Fertilization This usually happens between the thirteenth and fifteenth day of a woman's menstrual cycle and takes place in one of the *Fallopian tubes*. After it has been fertilized the *ovum* can begin to develop into a baby.

Fetus The name given to an unborn baby from two months after the start of a mother's pregnancy until it is born. (From fertilization to two months it is called an embryo.)

Fiber A substance that gives bulk to the diet. It is not digested, but it helps to keep the digestive system functioning healthily. Foods such as bran, whole wheat bread, and fruit are particularly high in fiber.

Fingerprints No two people, not even identical twins, have the same fingerprints, which is why the police use them as a sure means of identification. A developing baby's fingerprints are already formed after just 3 months in its mother's *womb*. Some genetic defects, such as Down's Syndrome, can be revealed from fingerprints. People with Down's Syndrome have looped fingerprint patterns. Fingerprints are

radial loop

whorl

double loops

arch

formed by tiny ridges in the epidermis. There are six patterns which are very common:

double loops	tented loops
radial loop	arch
whorl	ulnar loop

The study of fingerprint patterns is called "dermatoglyphics."

Follicle A small pocket in the skin from which a single hair grows.

Freckle A small light brown spot on the skin. Most freckles are on the face and arms. They are caused by a concentration of the pigment *melanin* in small groups of skin cells which reacts after the skin has been exposed to the sun's rays.

G

Gall bladder A small sac, about 3–4 inches (8–10cm) long, under the *liver*. The gall bladder releases the *bile* when fatty foods are in the *intestine*. Bile helps to digest fat.

Genes Combinations of *DNA* units which make up the individual *chromosomes* in each cell. Genes are inherited from parents and carry information about physical and certain emotional characteristics.

Glands The body has two types of glands. Exocrine glands, like the salivary glands in the mouth or sweat glands in the skin, produce substances which are carried away in ducts. *Endocrine* glands produce *hormones* which are secreted directly into the blood.

Glucose A sugar which can be carried in the blood. *Carbohydrate* foods are digested to form glucose. Glucose is broken down in the cells during *respiration* to release the energy you need to stay alive. It can be stored in the *liver* and muscles as glycogen which is easily converted back to glucose when the body needs extra energy.

H

Hemoglobin The red pigment found in *red blood cells* which gives blood its color. Hemoglobin carries oxygen from the lungs to the cells.

Hemophilia An inherited disorder in which blood clots very slowly and a small injury may cause the loss of a lot of blood. Bumps and bruises can be very serious to a hemophiliac. Women rarely suffer from this disorder themselves, but they can be carriers and pass it on to their sons.

Hepatitis An inflammation of the *liver* usually caused by a *virus*. The virus may either be caught by taking contaminated food or drink, from infected blood or blood products, or from unhygienic syringes.

Homeopathy A way of treating diseases developed in the early 1800s by a German doctor called Samuel Hahnemann.

Medicines are given to help the body to fight the disease rather than destroy the cause of the illness itself. Homeopathy involves taking very small amounts of medicines that produce symptoms of the illness being treated.

Hormones The body's chemical messengers – substances produced in tiny amounts in the *endocrine* glands. The hormones control many body processes. For example, *insulin* from the pancreas regulates the amount of sugar in the blood, hormones from the *pituitary* gland control growth, and *ovaries* produce sex hormones which give a woman her female appearance.

Hypothermia The lowering of a person's body temperature which occurs when he or she is very cold for too long. This may happen when someone is outside for a long time in extremely cold weather and is often called exposure. It can be very serious and a person can die of hypothermia. An old person may suffer from hypothermia because he has insufficient heating in his home.

I

The main endocrine (hormone) glands of the body.

Immunization A way of preventing certain diseases, usually by giving injections. The injections make the person's body produce *antibodies* to the disease which make him or her immune in the future. Small amounts of weakened or killed *bacteria* or *viruses* or their poisons are used in the *vaccines* which are injected.

Incisors The flat front teeth which cut food. There are four incisors in the upper jaw and four in the lower jaw.

Indigestion A stomachache or upset often caused when a person eats too fast or eats something (such as fried or spicy food) which disagrees with him or her.

Influenza (or flu) A disease caused by a *virus* which produces headaches, high temperatures, sore throats, aches and pains, and running nose. Mild flu is like a cold, but the disease can be much more serious. Flu is very infectious.

Insulin The *hormone* produced by the *pancreas* which controls the level of *glucose* (sugar) in the blood. People who produce too little insulin suffer from *diabetes*.

Intestine The long tube, beginning at the stomach and ending at the anus, in which food is digested.

Iris The colored part of the eye which surrounds the pupil.

J

Jaundice The yellowing of skin and of the whites of the eyes caused by breakdown of *red blood cells* (in babies), *liver* diseases, or blockage of the bile duct

(because of gallstones). (Yellow coloring is caused by the presence of bilirubin from bile in the blood.)

Joint The place where two bones meet. Joints are lined with *cartilage* and held in place by *ligaments*. Special fluid keeps them oiled so that they work smoothly. There are several different kinds of joint: hinge joints in the fingers and elbow, ball and socket joints at the hip and shoulder, sliding joints at the wrist, and pivotal joints at the joint between the head and neck.

The knee – a hinge joint.

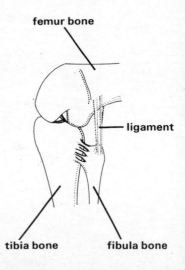

femur bone

ligament

tibia bone

fibula bone

K

Keratin The hard substance which is found in nails, hair, and skin.

Kidneys There are two kidneys, one on each side of the spine, just below the ribs. They filter waste from the blood and produce urine which collects in the *bladder*.

Leucocyte Another name for a *white blood cell*.

Leukemia A disease in which there is an excess of *white blood cells* in the blood. It is caused by *cancer* of the bone *marrow*.

Ligament A tough elastic band of tissue which holds bones together at a *joint*. If a joint is twisted out of place, ligaments are torn and a *sprain* occurs, which can cause considerable pain and swelling.

Liver The body's largest *gland*, shaped like a wedge. Digested food goes to the liver which

L

Lacrimal glands The glands above your eyes, under your eyelids, which produce tears. Tears keep the front of your eyes clean as you blink.

Larynx (voice box) Located at the top of the trachea, in the neck, it is made of cartilage and has *vocal cords* inside it. Air from your lungs makes the cords vibrate and muscles make the cords longer or shorter as you speak.

The lymphatic system.

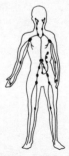

stores iron and some *glucose* (as glycogen) and processes *amino acids*, so that they can be used in other parts of the body. The liver also produces *bile*, a digestive juice which helps to digest *fats*. An adult's liver weighs about 3 pounds (1,500g).

Lymph A clear liquid which contains *white blood cells*. It flows in the lymphatic system and helps to fight disease and carry digested fats away from the small *intestine*.

Lymphocyte A type of *white blood cell* which has *antibodies* on its surface. In adults, a quarter of all white blood cells are lymphocytes. In children, the proportion is higher.

M

Malignant cells Slightly altered cells which grow faster than normal cells and form a cancerous *tumor* which damages other cells nearby. Malignant cells may leave one tumor and travel to other parts of the body where new tumors may grow. (The opposite of malignant is *benign*.)

Marrow A soft jelly-like substance in the hollow centers of some bones. It is made of blood vessels, *fats*, blood-producing cells, and developing *red* and *white blood cells*.

Medulla The base of the brain which joins the *spinal cord*. The word is also used to describe central areas in various other body organs.

Melanin The dark pigment which gives color to the skin, hair, and eyes.

Membranes Thin layers of cells which line or cover various parts of the body. Membranes line the nose, mouth, and intestine, and cover the heart, lungs, and other organs. Many lining membranes produce mucus to protect the body – in particular its openings – from infection.

Menopause The time when a woman stops having *periods* and releasing *ova* from her *ovaries*. This is usually between the ages of 45 and 55 years.

Menstruation (periods). Bleeding from the *vagina* as the lining of the *uterus* breaks down during the female menstrual cycle. The average time between one period and the next is 28 days, but this varies a great deal from person to person.

Microorganism Very tiny living things such as *viruses* and *bacteria* (often called germs) which can only be seen with the help of a microscope.

Mineral salts Substances which the body uses as raw materials. Iron is used to make *red blood cells*, calcium and phosphorus are used for bones and teeth, sodium and potassium are used in body fluids. Some mineral salts are needed in tiny amounts, such as iodine for the *thyroid* gland.

Molar teeth Large flat teeth at the back of the mouth used for grinding food.

Multiple sclerosis A disease in which the linings of nerves in certain parts of the brain and *spinal cord* are damaged. A person with this disease may suddenly become weak or have difficulty in walking or doing complicated work. The symptoms may disappear for a while but return after weeks, months, or sometimes years.

Muscle There are three types of muscles in the body: skeletal or striped muscle which allows for movement, heart muscle (or cardiac muscle) which pumps blood around the body, and smooth muscle which is found in tubes such as the *intestine* and moves food by *peristalsis*. Voluntary muscles are those which we can control; involuntary muscles, like the heart, function automatically.

Muscular dystrophy The name given to diseases in which a person's *muscles* waste away. Usually it begins in childhood and the person becomes gradually weaker and weaker until he or she cannot walk properly. Sufferers may also have respiratory problems. The cause of muscular dystrophy is not known, but it can be inherited, and boys and men are more often affected than women and girls.

Myelin The fatty "insulation" which covers the *nerve* fibers.

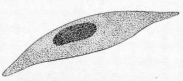

A (smooth) muscle cell.

N

Nerves Bundles of the long fibers of nerve cells which carry electrical messages to and from the brain and *spinal cord*. Each nerve cell has a body and a long fiber coming from it. If the body of the cell is damaged it cannot be replaced, although damaged fibers can regrow. There are two types of nerve cells. Sensory cells transmit messages to the brain and motor cells carry messages away from the brain.

Neuron Another word for a nerve cell.

O

Organ A group of different tissues which work together to perform a special job in the body, for example the *kidneys*, heart, and lungs.

Ovaries The two female organs which produce ova. One is released each month from *puberty* to *menopause* (about 11 years to 45–55 years). Ovaries are about 1½ inches (4cm) long and are in the lower part of a woman's abdomen.

Ovum Another word for an egg cell.

P

Pancreas A 6 inch (15cm) long *gland* behind the stomach. It produces the hormone *insulin,* which controls the body's blood sugar level, and pancreatic juice, which helps to digest food in the *duodenum* (small intestine).

Pediatrics The branch of medicine which deals with children's development and the treatment of their illnesses from birth to early teens.

Pelvis The hip bones which protect the abdomen, support the base of the spine, and provide a place for the attachment of the legs. A woman's pelvis is wider than a man's to allow for the development of a baby.

An ovum (egg) cell.

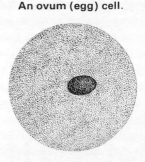

Penicillin An antibiotic produced by a mold (fungus). It kills or damages certain disease-producing *bacteria* – for example, pneumococcus, which causes *pneumonia*.

Periods see *menstruation*.

Peristalsis The waves of contraction in the walls of tubes in the body to move substances along. Food moves along the *intestine* by peristalsis.

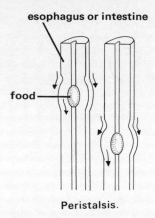

Peristalsis.

Phagocyte A *white blood cell* that engulfs *bacteria*.

Physiotherapy The treatment of an injury by exercise, massage, or heat to help muscles and joints start working again.

Pituitary gland The *endocrine* gland at the base of the brain which produces and releases several *hormones*, including growth hormones, hormones which stimulate the *thyroid* gland, oxytocin which controls birth, and hormones which stimulate the *ovaries* and *testes* to make hormones of their own. Because the pituitary gland controls other glands it is often called the master gland.

Placenta The tissue which develops in the *uterus* during pregnancy. One side of it is attached to the *uterus* wall and the other is connected to the developing baby by the *umbilical cord*. The baby receives food and oxygen through the placenta and returns carbon dioxide and waste to its mother's blood. The placenta also produces *hormones* which control the pregnancy.

Plasma The liquid part of blood which remains when *red* and *white blood cells* and platelets are removed.

Plastic surgery Surgery which repairs or rebuilds parts of the body which have been damaged or scarred. Doctors may use skin grafts or artificial parts in order to do this.

Pneumonia A disease in which the lungs become inflamed and the air sacs fill with fluid, making it difficult to breathe. There are two types of pneumonia, one is caused by a *virus* and the other by a *bacterium*. If both lungs are affected, the disease is called "double pneumonia."

Polio An infection of the *central nervous system*. It is caused by a *virus*. Most children are immunized against this disease.

Progesterone A female *hormone* which stimulates the thickening of the lining of the *uterus*.

Proteins Body-building chemicals which are part of every living cell. Proteins are made of subunits called *amino acids*. When you eat food containing protein it is digested into amino acids which build new proteins in your cells. Foods which contain protein include fish, meat, eggs, milk, and beans.

Puberty The time when the reproductive system becomes active. Puberty begins between 12–15 years for a boy and between 10–14 years for a girl.

Pulmonary artery The main artery from the right *ventricle* to the lungs. The blood which it carries is low in oxygen but contains a lot of carbon dioxide.

Pulmonary vein The main vein from the lungs to the left *atrium* of the heart. It carries blood which contains a lot of oxygen.

Pulse The throbbing which can be felt in arteries as the heart pumps. The pulse can be felt most strongly in your wrist. The number of beats per minute is your pulse rate. For adults this is 65–80 beats per minute, for a 10-year-old about 90 beats per minute, and for a baby about 140 beats per minute.

Pupil The black opening in the center of the *iris* through which light enters the eye.

R

Rectum The last section of the large *intestine* just before the anus.

Red blood cells The small disk-shaped cells in the blood which carry oxygen to all cells. Red blood cells contain *hemoglobin* which gives them their red color.

Reflex actions Those which are automatic and cannot be controlled by thinking about them, for example, the knee-jerk reflex.

Renal Referring to the *kidneys*; for example, the renal *artery*.

Respiration The process of using oxygen in cells to release energy from *glucose* and the release of carbon dioxide. Respiration is also used to mean breathing.

S

The path of a reflex response.

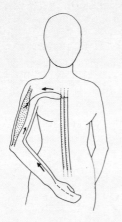

Retina The inner lining of the eyeball which is sensitive to light. Light rays enter the eye through the *pupil* and are focused onto the retina by the lens. Cells in the retina respond to the light by sending messages to the brain.

Rod A light-sensitive receptor cell in the retina which responds to give black-and-white vision.

Rubella Another name for German measles – a disease caused by a *virus* which produces a pink rash on the face, neck, and body. It is usually not a very serious illness, but if a pregnant woman should catch it, her baby may be born with defects. Most girls are given injections to immunize them against rubella when they are about 13 years old.

Saliva The liquid produced by three pairs of *glands* in the mouth. Saliva moistens food so that it can be swallowed easily and it contains an *enzyme* (ptyalin) which digests starch. More saliva is produced as you eat, although a little is produced all the time.

Sebaceous gland An oil-producing *gland* in the skin.

Serum The yellow watery liquid left when all the blood cells, platelets, and clotting agents have been removed from blood. It is *plasma* minus clotting agents.

Siamese twins Identical twins who are joined together when they are born. Often they are joined at the head, chest, or hips. They can be separated unless they share one important *organ* such as the heart.

Sinuses Four sets of hollow cavities inside the skull. There are two in the forehead, one behind the nasal passages and one in the cheeks. They warm the air which you breathe in. When the *membranes* which line the cavities are infected the illness is called "sinusitis."

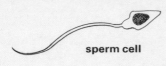
sperm cell

Sneeze A *reflex* action which forces air out of the lungs through the nose in order to clear an irritation in the nasal passages. Sneezing is a common way of spreading infection because tiny droplets of mucus which contain *bacteria* are also sneezed out.

Sperm The male sex cells which are produced in the *testes* of a man. If a sperm cell meets and fertilizes an *ovum* (egg cell) a new baby can develop. Sperm carry genetic information.

Sphincter A round band of *muscle* fibers at the entrance or exit to an *organ*. Sphincter muscles can close the exit from the *bladder*, from the *rectum* to the anus, and the exit from the stomach into the *duodenum*.

Spina bifida A birth defect in which bones of the spine do not protect the *spinal cord*. The spinal cord may also be deformed and some nerves may be missing (spina bifida means "divided spine"). About 1 in 500 babies have spina bifida. Now tests can be done during pregnancy to detect a baby with spina bifida before it is born.

Spinal cord The thick cord of nerves (nervous tissue) which begins at the base of the brain and extends to the bottom of the back. *Nerves* branching off it go to different parts of the body. It is enclosed and protected inside the vertebrae of your spine.

Spleen A soft organ which weighs about 8 ounces (227g) found on the left side of the body between the stomach and *diaphragm*. In developing babies the spleen makes *red blood cells*. In adults it is part of the *lymph* system and helps fight infection, as well as remove worn-out red cells from the blood.

Sprain A sharp painful twisting of a *joint* which damages the *ligaments* holding it in place.

Synapse The minute gap between the *axon* of one *neuron* and a *dendrite* of the next. A special substance called a "neurotransmitter" fills the gap for an instant so that the message which a *nerve* carries can cross it.

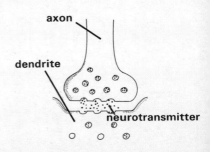

T

Tendons Very strong bands of tissue which connect *muscles* to bones. As muscles contract, tendons pull bones so that you can move.

Testes The two male sex *glands* which produce *sperm* cells and male *hormones*. They are held just outside the abdomen in a pouch which is called the "scrotum."

Tetanus A serious disease caused by Clostridium *bacteria* found in the soil. It causes muscles to have spasms and contract involuntarily. (Often the first muscles to be affected are those in the jaw, hence the other name for the disease – "lockjaw.") The bacteria get into the body through wounds and cuts, especially if they become dirty with soil.

Most children are *immunized* against tetanus and doctors give an anti-tetanus injection as a precaution if a person cuts himself or herself badly.

Thorax The airtight cavity which contains the heart and lungs and is enclosed by the *diaphragm* underneath and the ribs at the sides.

Thymus A *gland* in the lower neck. In young people it produces *antibodies* and *white blood cells* to help fight infection. It becomes smaller in adults.

Thyroid A *gland* in the neck, on both sides of the *trachea,* which produces the *hormone* thyroxine. Thyroxine controls the growth rate and the speed of chemical processes in the body.

Tissues Groups of similar cells which form various parts of the body. *Nerve* tissue, made of many nerve cells, can conduct messages. *Muscles* are another kind of tissue which can contract and skin is a tissue made of many flat cells.

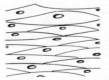

Smooth muscle tissue.

177

Tonsils Oval structures found at the entrance to the throat. Together with the *adenoids* they guard against the *bacteria* which may enter through the mouth and nose. "Tonsillitis" is an infection in the tonsils. Sometimes tonsils are removed if they become infected repeatedly.

Trachea (or windpipe) The tube which leads from the *larynx* in the throat to the two main *bronchi* in the chest. The trachea has incomplete rings of *cartilage* to keep it open all the time.

Transplants A transplant occurs when a doctor is able to replace a diseased or damaged *organ* with a healthy one from another person. Parts of the body which have been successfully transplanted are the heart and bone *marrow*, the *cornea* of the eye, *kidneys*, *liver*, and lungs. The blood and *tissue* types of donors and the person who receives the transplant must be carefully matched so that the immune system of the recipient does not reject the new part. The chance of rejection can be reduced if the recipient takes drugs which suppress his or her immune system.

Tumor A swelling caused by the abnormal growth of cells without a useful function. There are two kinds of tumor, *benign* and *malignant*.

Tympanum see *eardrum*.

U

Ulcer An open sore on the skin or on a membrane inside the body. There are many different kinds of ulcers. Mouth ulcers form inside the mouth if it is scratched or injured. Stomach ulcers and *duodenal* ulcers develop in the *intestine* as gastric juices begin to digest its walls. People who worry a lot tend to develop these types of ulcers. Nearly all of them heal by themselves.

Umbilical cord The cord which connects a developing baby to the *placenta* inside its mother's *uterus*. The cord contains two *arteries* and one *vein* and through these the baby receives nourishment and gets rid of waste.

When a baby is born its umbilical cord is about 18 inches (45cm) long. A doctor or midwife cuts the cord and leaves a stump about 2 inches (6cm) long attached to the baby. This falls off after a week or two, leaving the navel or "belly button" where it was attached.

Ureters The tubes which carry urine from the *kidneys* to the *bladder*. They are about 12 inches (30cm) long, but very narrow, only $\frac{1}{25}$th of an inch (0.01cm) in some places.

Urethra The tube which leads from the *bladder* to the outside of the body. Females have a shorter urethra than males because the male urethra reaches to the tip of his penis.

Uterus (womb) The part of a woman's body, inside her abdomen, where a baby grows and develops.

V

Vaccination Injecting a person with weakened or dead disease-causing microorganisms. Vaccination is the injection itself, *immunization* is the effect that vaccination causes.

Vagina The passageway from the *uterus* to the outside of a woman's body. It is about 4–5inches (10–12cm) long and is made of *muscle* lined with a *membrane*. During childbirth it stretches to let the baby out.

Varicose veins Veins which have become weakened so that their walls are stretched and their valves have difficulty stopping blood from flowing the wrong way. Often this happens in the legs of people who stand up a lot. Varicose veins in the *rectum* are called "hemorrhoids" or "piles."

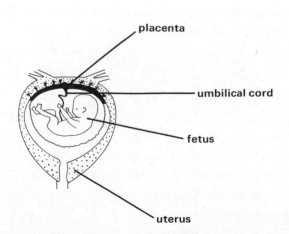

placenta

umbilical cord

fetus

uterus

Vein Any blood vessel which carries blood toward the heart.

Venae cavae The main *veins* which carry blood to the right *atrium* of the heart.

Ventricle The two larger, lower chambers of the heart. The right ventricle pumps blood to the lungs and the left ventricle pumps blood around the body.

Verruca The medical name for a wart. Verrucas are small, hard growths on the skin. They usually occur on feet and hands and are caused by a *virus*. They are common in children and young people.

Villi Tiny, finger-like projections from the linings of the small *intestine* which absorb digested food.

Viruses Microorganisms which cause many diseases if they infect the body. Different viruses cause colds, chicken pox, measles, mumps, and polio.

Vitamins A group of substances found in food which are essential for health. You need small amounts of about 15 different vitamins so that chemical processes can take place in your body. A lack of any one vitamin can cause illness. For example a lack of vitamin D can cause children to develop "rickets," a disorder of the bones.

Vocal cords Two *ligaments* stretched across the *larynx*. They are controlled by *muscles* which vary the length and tension of the cords so that you can speak as air passes over them and makes them vibrate.

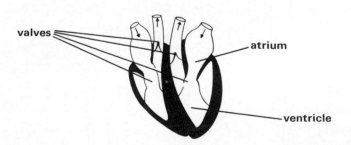

Arrows indicate direction of blood through the heart.

W

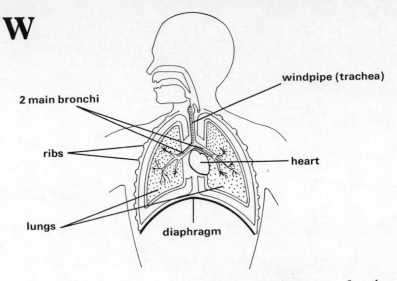

2 main bronchi

windpipe (trachea)

ribs

heart

lungs

diaphragm

Wart see *verruca*.

White blood cells Colorless cells in blood which help to fight disease. They are larger than *red blood cells* and are made in the bone *marrow*.

Whooping cough A serious infection of the *bronchi* and lungs. It is like a heavy cold, with a temperature and cough which gets worse until the person begins to "whoop" and has difficulty in breathing. This disease is most common in children under 10 years. It can be prevented by a vaccine.

Windpipe Another name for the *trachea*, the air passage which connects the throat to the bronchi and lungs.

Womb Another name for the *uterus*, the hollow organ in a woman's *pelvis* where a fertilized *ovum* develops into a baby.

Y

Yawning A *reflex* action in which the mouth is opened wide and a breath is slowly released. You may yawn because you need fresh air, because you are tired, or because of a combination of these reasons. You may also yawn when you see someone else do so although no one knows why yawning seems to be so infectious.

Index

Page numbers in **bold**
type refer to main entries
in glossary; page numbers
in *italic* type refer to
illustrations.

\

A

Abcess, **152**
Acne, 39, **152**
Actin, *25*
Acupuncture, **152**, *153*
Adam's apple, 80, **152**
Adenine, *111*
Adenoids, *95*, **152**
ADH, 89
Adipose tissue, *36*, 37
Adolescence, 40, 122–3
ADP, *76*
Adrenal glands, *88*, 91,
   159
Adrenalin, 91, **152**
Afterbirth, 108
Aging *see* Older people
Aldosterone, 91
Allergy, 96, **152**, 155, 163
Alveoli, 76, *77*, 79, 81,
   154, *154*
Ambidexterity, 120
Amino acids, 66, 72, 82,
   85, **154**
Amnion, 106
Amniotic fluid, 106, *107*
Anemia, 69, **154**
Anesthetics, 142–3, *143*,
   146, 152, **154**
Anorexia nervosa, **154**
Antibiotics, 101, 148,
   154–5, 173
Antibodies, 33, 94, 96,
   155, 169, 177
Antiseptics, 144, **155**
Anus, 70, *71*, 72, 176
Anvil, 54, *54*
Aorta, *29*, 30, *31*, **155**
Appendicitis, 73, 101, 155
Appendix, *71*, 73, **155**
Arteries, 28, *29*, **155**, 158,
   178; hardening, 34, 159;
   heart and lung, 30, *31*,
   32, 34, 35

Arthritis, 92, 124
Arthroscope, 11
Asthma, **155**
Athlete's foot, **155**
ATP, *76*
Atria, 30, *31*, 32, **155**
Auricles, *see* Atria
Autonomic Nervous
   System, 42, 47, **155**
Axon, 44–5, *45*, **155**

B

Babies, 69, 74, 79, 86,
   168, 174; birth, 89, 108,
   109, 125, 158, 178,
   179; development, 118–
   20, *118*, *119*, *128*;
   unborn, 106, *107*, 159,
   175, 176, 178; ('test
   tube'), 151
Backbone *see* Vertebrae
Bacteria, 35, 100, 152,
   154–5, **156**, *156*; and
   antibiotics, 101, 148,
   173; in food, 69, 70, 75,
   164; and immune
   system, 92–9, *93*, 162,
   177; studies, 144, 145,
   149
Balance, 47, 54, 57
Baldness, 40
Barium meal, 147
Barnard, Christiaan, 150,
   150
BCG, **156**
Biceps, *22*, *23*, **157**
Bile, 73, **157**, 168
Bionic arm, 151
Birth, 89, 108, *109*, 158,
   178, 179; rate, 125
Bladder, 82, *83*, 85, 86
Blindness, 62, *132*; color,
   61, 116
Blind spot, 59, **157**
Blood, 15, 28–35, *29*, 42,
   141, *141*, cells: (red),
   21, 28, *28*, 35, 67, 73,
   77, 85, 94, **174**; (white),

15, 28, *28*, 35, 85, 94,
   181; clotting, 20, 33, 34,
   35, 68; groups, 33, 115,
   148; poisoning, 35;
   pressure, 28, 34, 47, 69,
   92, **157**; supply to
   organs *see* under names
   of organs
Blundell, James, 148
Blushing, **157**
Body scanner, *11*, 150
Boils, 93, 152
Bone, 10, *16*, 17–22, 118,
   121, 124; cells, 15, 20;
   fractures, 20, *20*, 92;
   joints *see* Joints;
   marrow, 21, *21*, 28, 94,
   170
Bowel, **157**
Bowman's capsule, *84*, 85
Brain, 42–9, *43*, *47*, *48*,
   89, 124; activity, *49*,
   125, 148; cells, 14, 35,
   90; and heart, 32; and
   hormones, 89; and
   memory, 124, 130–1,
   137; and senses, 50, 52,
   57, 124; (sight), 58, 59,
   61, 130–1, 162
Breasts, 92, 118, 123, 172
Breathing *see* Respiration
Bronchi, 76, *77*, 79, **157**
Bronchioles, 76, *77*
Bronchitis, 79, 125, 157
Bronchoscope, 10
Bruises, 34, 35, **157**

C

Caesarian section, 108,
   158
Calcium, 17, 21, 34, 67,
   89
Calmette-Guerin, Bacille,
   156
Calories, 67
Cancer, 79, 92, 125, 148,
   158, 169
Canines, 74, *74*, 120, **158**

183

185

ACKNOWLEDGEMENTS

Photographs: page 10 Middlesex Hospital; 11 *top* EMI Medical Ltd, *bottom* Coherent UK Ltd; 14 Gene Cox; 18 Middlesex Hospital; 24 Gene Cox; 27 The Big Apple Health Studio; 33 National Blood Transfusion Service; 37 Zefa; 65 J. Allan Cash Ltd; 79 Gene Cox; 85 Middlesex Hospital; 87 Elga Ltd; 90 British Diabetic Association; 93 Gene Cox; 96 World Health Organisation; 101 *left* Dolland & Aitchison, *right* Glasgow Dental School; 103 Zefa; 105 Medical Research Council; 106 Sonotron Medical Electronics; 108–118 Zefa; 121 Middlesex Hospital; 122 & 124 Zefa; 132 Royal National Institute For The Blind; 133 Zefa; 134 British Museum; 135 National Gallery; 136 NASA; 137 Science Photo Library; 139 Maritshius, The Hague; 140 & 141 Mansell; 145 Mary Evans; 146 Mansell; 147 & 148 BBC Hulton; 149 Picturepoint; 150 Camera Press; 151 Popperfoto; 165 Metropolitan Police.

Picture Research: Penny J. Warn.